*G*ender stereotypes and bias hurt bc

- *Boys who like to read.*
- *Boys who don't like hunting, fishing, or mechanics.*
- *Boys who don't like sports (or who do, but are pushed too hard).*

*G*ender stereotypes and bias also hurt girls:

- *Girls who aren't shown positive female role models in textbooks.*
- *Girls who are discouraged from excelling at traditionally male–dominated sports.*
- *Girls who try to achieve an impossibly ideal body image.*

It's time to expand society's code of conduct to be more fair. Gender equity means greater freedom for individuals—both boys and girls— to be themselves.

Gender bias hurts everyone.

Beyond Dolls & Guns

Beyond
Dolls & Guns

101 Ways to Help Children Avoid Gender Bias

Susan Hoy Crawford

Heinemann
Portsmouth, NH

HEINEMANN
A division of Reed Elsevier Inc.
361 Hanover Street   Portsmouth, NH 03801-3912
Offices and agents throughout the world

The author and publisher are grateful for permission to reprint previously published
material. Credit lines appear in text.

Library of Congress Cataloging-in-Publication Data
Crawford, Susan Hoy.
    Beyond dolls & guns : 101 ways to help children avoid
gender bias / by Susan Hoy Crawford.
        p.   cm.
    Includes bibliographical references.
    ISBN 0–435–08129–2
    1. Sex role in children. 2. Sexism. 3. Child rearing.
4. Identity (Psychology) in children. I. Title.
HQ784.S45C73   1995
649'.1—dc20   95–31952
                                                    CIP

Editor: Cheryl Kimball
Production: J. B. Tranchemontagne
Design: Mary Cronin
Cover design: Darci Mehall
Printed in the United States of America on acid-free paper

99 98 97 96 DA 9 8 7 6 5 4 3 2 1

To the late Myra Pollack Sadker, who recognized the need for and encouraged the writing of this book.

Dr. Sadker was a pioneer of gender equity in education, an accomplished researcher and author, and a generous, gifted educator.

and to today's busy, hardworking, thoughtful parents

Contents

Acknowledgments

There are so many people who have shown extraordinary generosity toward this project that I would like to thank. It is impossible in a book of this type to mention everyone by name, but I would like to express my deep gratitude:

to the generous leading educators and experts who read manuscript drafts; gave their valuable time, attention, insights, and wisdom; and whose foresight leads the way;

to the tirelessly cheerful reference librarians who helped procure needed documents and offered valuable judgments and assistance;

to the inspirational organizations who advocate for justice and better education for the nation's children, for their leadership, vital work, trust, and prompt support;

to devoted friends and family who contributed their support, candid assessments, time, and professional skills so generously;

to my editors, whose dedicated efforts helped to make this a better book;

to my daughters Katie and Evelyn and our friend Duncan, whose experiences provided inspiration for this book and many of its examples;

and especially to my husband Jay, who supported me during the writing of this book in so many ways, including contribution of his professional talents.

Although I have grouped people together I remember each person's unique contribution and I offer to every one heartfelt thanks and appreciation.

LUANN © 1993 Greg Evans. Reprinted with special permission of North America Syndicate.

How to Use This Book

In order to use this book, particularly in the context of parent/school interactions, it is important to understand the meaning of some important terms. Most of the expressions listed below continue to evolve, so definitions of what they mean in this book have been provided. There are two terms that it is most important for parents with children in public schools to understand: *discrimination* and *bias*. *Discrimination* is illegal under Federal Civil Rights Law Title IX. *Bias* is not. The distinction is particularly important when parents approach school officials on issues relating to sexism.

Sexism: *n* 1. attitudes or behavior based on traditional stereotypes of sexual roles 2. discrimination or devaluation based on a person's sex, as in restricted job opportunities.

Discrimination: *n* 1. an act of discriminating 2. treatment or consideration of, or making a distinction in favor of or against a person or thing based on the group, class, or category to which that person or thing belongs rather than on individual merit.

Bias: *n* a particular tendency or inclination, especially one that prevents unprejudiced consideration of a question; prejudice.

Fair: *adj.* (as the term is currently applied in the education world) 1. legitimately done under the rules 2. treating all in the same way.

Examples: equally allotted treatment by and/or interactions with a teacher; equally administered disciplinary consequences.

Affirmative: *adj.* 1. affirming or assenting; asserting the truth, validity, or fact of something; a positive statement or proposition; affirmation 2. as the term is currently applied in the education world, attempts to compensate for effects of current societal/curriculum bias or past discrimination. Examples: deliberately working to change play and seating patterns if children are consistently choosing stereotypic activities and same-gender partners; encouraging students to consider both boys and girls for a leadership position during class elections, evaluating assumptions reflected in electing males to be president and females to be secretary; or, deliberately reversing the sex-role stereotypes, encouraging girls to participate in team sports and boys to engage in nurturing activities.

In public education, discrimination has a legal meaning that has been established by the court system on the basis of court cases challenged, won, and lost. Parents will want to be very careful about the way they use this term with school officials. Discrimination, for public schools and institutions of higher education that receive federal funding, has been defined under Title IX of the Civil Rights Act of 1972. Title IX simply says:

> No person in the United States shall, on the basis of sex, be excluded from participation in, be denied the benefits of, or be subjected to discrimination under any program or activity receiving Federal financial assistance.

Within school programs and environments this has come to be defined by court challenges in two ways:

- **Equal access**
- **Equal treatment**

Equal access means that a student may not be denied access to any class or program on the basis of gender. This means that boys are no longer barred from home economics classes, and girls are allowed to take Shop and classes in automotive repair. It also means, by the way, that girls may not be barred from contact sports just because they are girls. If there is only one team, and the girl presents a letter from her doctor stating that she is big enough and strong enough (there are size/weight tables for qualification) she must be allowed to try out, regardless of gender.

Equal treatment refers to stated policies and funding. If a boy is suspended for smoking, for example, then the same disciplinary policy must apply to a girl who is caught smoking. In terms of policies (discipline, dress codes, guidance counseling) students must be treated equally, regardless of gender. EQUAL FUNDING of programs is also important in facilitating Equal access and Equal treatment. If there are ten sports programs offered for boys, and only three offered for girls, girls are denied access via unequal funding. While it is considered okay for different sports to incur unequal costs because of differences in equipment, something like equipment replacement schedules should be based on the same criteria for both sexes. If the boys' basketball team gets new shirts every year, then so should the girls' basketball team, as the equipment (in this case, shirts) receives equal wear and tear.

As parents look around their children's schools, they may find that what they thought was discrimination does not fit the above categories. Public schools are supposed to have a designated local Title IX administrator who conducts periodic reviews to assure that compliance with Title IX is ongoing; and parents may ask to see these assessments. Parents may also challenge the school district on compliance matters via a Title IX complaint to the Federal Office of Civil Rights. Most schools comply, or are close to compliance, on Title IX requirements. Unless a state, a school district, or a college has additional stated policies of its own, or unless the courts decide that Title IX means more or less than the above, parent-identified sexism may not violate any policy or law. Most unequal treatment in school currently falls into the gender bias category. Bias can be demonstrated in teacher interactions, in curriculum, and in lack of school policies. Thus it is possible for a teacher to be absolutely fair in administering a biased curriculum.

Some schools and states already have policies that target all types of gender bias. The best of these policies have been specific about goals, have established timetables for action plans, and have set deadlines for compliance assessments. Other schools, however, have not addressed sexism in the form of gender bias—or in any other form—for many years. The tests in Chapter 1, the examples, and the terms will help parents determine whether sexism is in evidence and how to describe it so it can be eliminated.

Parts of the Book

- **Chapter 1** offers advice on how to identify gender bias in a child's environment.

- **Chapters 2 through 7** are a checklist of ideas and action steps for adults to help them counteract society's gender stereotypes. Busy adults can read these in any order they wish. The tips are numbered sequentially for ease of reference and divided into chapters by subject. Tips that apply to younger children are generally located toward the beginning of each chapter, and those for older children toward the end.

- **Appendixes** containing Non-Biased, Inclusive Language; Research Summaries; Famous Women in History; and Bibliography of Non-sexist Children's and Adult Reference Books put reference information in an easy-to-use form.

Doonesbury

BY GARRY TRUDEAU

DON'T WE HAVE A PARENTS' OPEN CLASS TODAY?

IT WAS YESTERDAY, DURING YOUR SHIFT. DON'T WORRY, ALEX IS DOING FINE.

4-27

YEAH, WELL, I'D LIKE TO SEE FOR MYSELF. I WANT TO MAKE SURE OUR DAUGHTER ISN'T GETTING A GIRL'S EDUCATION!

A GIRL'S EDUCATION?

OKAY, WHO KNOWS THE ANSWER? JASON? ANDREW? JONATHAN? NICHOLAS?

MAYBE IF I WORE BRIGHTER COLORS...

Introduction

By far the most prevalent crippling disease—
for both boys and girls—
is sex stereotyping.
                    —Dr. Benjamin Spock

Formidable words from America's most trusted child-raising expert. And he is not alone. Monthly, it seems, there are new headlines in newspapers and magazines or new TV reports heralding the results of recent studies (see appendixes for summaries of current research):

- Girls' Self-Esteem—High in Elementary, Low by High School

- Girls Face Sexual Harassment in School, Even in Youngest Grades

- Girls' Math and Science Scores—High in Elementary, Plummet in High School

- Boys in Gangs Molest Girls—Later Brag of Achievements and Initiation Rites

- Boys in School and American Society—The Violence is Increasing

Educators are talking about gender equity issues. Baby Boomer parents, who have come to expect fairness in the workplace, are seeing their children face the same stereotypes at school and on the playground that they faced as children.

Dr. Spock has revised his famous book, *Baby and Child Care,* to include several new sections: "The Subordination of Women Is Brought on by Countless Small Acts Beginning in Early Childhood," "Discrimination Is Still Rampant," and "Men Need Liberating, Too."

Popular books document problems that adolescent girls face, including research that adolescent girls suffer more psychologically than adolescent boys do. Adolescent girls lose self-confidence and the pressure of social conformity robs their mental energy from other work. Girls often learn to dislike other women as well as themselves when they see that women in our society are less respected than men. Girls suffer when girls' sports are considered second class or when they are discouraged from activities that develop observable muscles. Girls still face a limited choice of careers where they will be expected or even welcome. Girls face the added pressure to compete with boys when they grow up, but without confidence-building role models: women and their many major contributions to this country have simply been left out of textbooks. Girls suffer physically as they starve and paint themselves to achieve artificial, perfect beauty. And girls continue to suffer the double standard in terms of sexuality.

While there are some who feel that gender equity means boys will have to lose the advantages they now enjoy, many adults know that sexism hurts boys, too. The boy who likes quiet, contemplative activities like poetry, writing, music, or art. The boy who likes theater. The boy who doesn't like hunting or fishing or who is mechanically inept. The boy who doesn't like to fight or thinks fighting isn't a very good way to resolve problems. The boy who doesn't like gang dynamics, but isn't able to change the behavior of the pack. The boy who would like to play with his friend, who happens to be a girl, but doesn't dare risk it. Though less acknowledged by the media, sexism is hurting boys as individuals and their gender as a whole by limiting their range of experiences, and thus their growth.

Gender inequities affect so many children. We have all spoken the phrase "women and minorities." Paired in this way, these words suggest that women are a peripheral group. Some people even say "women and other minorities." But women are not a minority. Women (and girls) are the majority, 51 to 53 percent of the population, depending on who is doing the counting. If we add the number of boys who are negatively affected by sexual stereotypes to the number of girls in the population, we are clearly talking about the majority of children. This is a problem that needs addressing.

Leading educators have begun formulating plans to address gender equity issues. They are doing so for two reasons. First, they realize that they can improve the learning potential of most of their students by creating a fairer and more welcoming environment. Second, in analyzing the skills that will be required of today's students in the next century, they realize that those skills traditionally labeled feminine—communication, negotiation, interdependence—must be fostered in all students. Our co-ed educational system, devised over a century ago to educate boys, has simply added girls to the extant structure, which continues to foster hierarchical competition instead of teamwork, rote memory instead of creative problem solving, and compartmentalized learning instead of interdisciplinary knowledge. Educators and business leaders have come to realize that the model must change in order to prepare children for their twenty-first century future.

Our country's leaders have been pointing out for the last decade that we are entering an information age of high technology and service industries. Those hardest hit by unemployment are—and will continue to be—unskilled workers. We know that our children will probably have multiple careers, and that they will have to be flexible in their thinking and able to get along with all types of people. One of the messages of the past three decades—following the women's movement and the civil rights movement—is that we *need* women and that we *need* minorities in the workplace. We need the best minds and the best skills in order to participate in the new global community. We haven't a person to waste.

Those who have always felt that gender stereotypes were limiting and didn't fit them already know that examining gender bias is well worth the effort. Others, for whom the stereotypes feel natural, may have assumed that they *are* natural for the entire human species, for their children and everyone else. Hopefully those who sense that stereotypes feel right for themselves will be sensitive that they may not be so for many others, including children.

Individuals can alter their view of the world and the people around them. And they can alter the way they interact with the culture, on both the private and the public policy level. While many blatant sexual stereotypes have been retired, an abundance of subtle biases remain. Girls and boys *are* still being raised in separate societies, which is not helpful in preparing them for their future together. What can we do to help? Here are several suggestions:

- We can help our children to learn a variety of interests and skills.

  - We can consider the traits we want our children to have—such as honesty, competence, independence, respect for others, and self–reliance—and encourage them in all children. We need to support children as they explore all areas of learning and life.

- We can attempt to improve the social environment that surrounds our children.

  - We can create a network of safe adults around our children who will mentor them and encourage them to be themselves: self–assured, even *loud* girls (if that is who they are) and perceptive, even *quiet* boys (if that is who they are).

  - We can monitor ourselves when we are with children to prevent inequities in our interactions with them—in the time we give them to speak, in the type and amount of help we give them, and in the words we choose to use.

  - We can be alert in our interactions and conversations with other adults so that we do not perpetuate gender stereotyping.

  - We can lobby for public policy that identifies gender fairness as a goal. We can share our interest with other adults and join together to ask school boards, library boards, and male and female elected representatives to support gender equity goals, studies, projects, and legislation.

- We can do more to provide children with female role models and with mentors who demonstrate strength, intelligence, and power in their lives. And we can strive to show them male role models who nurture their own and others' humanity.

- We can give our children an awareness of what is inequitable and then teach them survival skills for coping with inequities so that they don't think the problem is within themselves.

Toward this end, this book offers a checklist of ideas and a number of resources that adults will find useful.

So, let us celebrate *human* accomplishments! Let us cherish each individual. Let us allow active children to be free to be energetic, regardless of gender. Let us encourage children who are socially aware, contemplative, and effective communicators to be free to be so, regardless of gender. Let us free children to be themselves and to pursue their many interests in an environment that rewards talent, honors diverse perspectives, and rejoices in the riches of true friendship and teamwork.

Legend

 Connotes an **Action Tip**

 Additional Reading on the subject

 Where to Call, Buy,* Lobby for faster progress

*All sources listed by the author are, without exception, unsolicited endorsements provided solely for the reader's convenience.

You're fooling yourself if you think you've got new and improved males because you see three or four dudes out there doing diapers and dishes.

—Bill Cosby

one

Is It
Sexism?

What you will find in this chapter:

- Help in identifying whether a situation in your child's environment is sexist

- Terms that can be used with educators in talking about bias

1. A quick check for determining whether a situation is sexist or not is *the racism test*. Simply substitute characters or terms that apply to different racial groups and see whether the same situation would be an example of racism.

Unless the situation has something to do with reproductive anatomy and its function, this test will help identify situations in which separate–but–equal assumptions are still present. Different religious groups, such as Christians and Jews, can also be substituted.

For example, a young boy announces at nursery or elementary school that he "hates girls" and refuses to play with them. Many adults would accept this as normal behavior and ignore it.

Framing this situation as the racism or black–and–white test—the child is white and announces that he "hates blacks" and refuses to play with them—it is clearly racist, and chances are that some adult will take the child aside, attempt to learn the source of such a socially unacceptable attitude, and try to encourage change.

2. Another test for sexism is a civil rights *workplace test*. Try substituting a public classroom situation for an office situation. Would the childhood social practice be legal and appropriate if it occurred in corporate America?

Let's say that you receive from school, a telephone and address list of your child's classmates, with the girls' names and the boys' names in two separate columns.

Now imagine a list of the telephone extensions of employees in a corporation, men in one column, women in another. This is clearly sexist and would be grounds for a lawsuit if it occurred in an American corporation.

3. A third test for sexual stereotypes and sexism is *the role reversal test.* Simply envision the same situation and reverse the gender roles. Is the meaning the same? Unless the subject has something to do with reproductive anatomy and its function, there should be no difference in meaning if the example is nonsexist.

If reversing the sexes of the characters makes the example seem odd or ludicrous, it is because sexual stereotypes have been assumed, thus illustrating bias.

Try reversing the sexes of the characters in *Sleeping Beauty:* "The prince pricks his finger on a spindle . . . and is saved in the end by a dragon-fighting princess."

Try changing the sexes in a toy commercial: Yelling, bounding girls crash their toy army jeeps into the "bad gal" enemy as they roar explosion noises.

Try another commercial: Substitute a woman giving a testimonial about the effectiveness of a mouthwash for a man doing the same. There is no difference in meaning, because either could be expected to occupy that role.

4. Look for the *quantity* of messages about girls and boys as well as the quality. You will begin to note *exclusion* or *invisibility,* one of the most common forms of bias.

Girl characters are often omitted in books, TV, and moviesin spite of the fact that they comprise half the child population. This in itself is a message to children.

Reflect on the characters in "Sesame Street": Bert, Ernie, Big Bird, Oscar, Elmo, Herry, Grover, the Count, Cookie Monster, Mr. Snuffle–upagus . . . and Prairie Dawn and Zoe? How about Winnie-the-Pooh? Christopher Robin, Tigger, Eeyore, Piglet, Owl, Rabbit, Roo. The only female is the mother, Kanga.

The significant omission of women (and people of color) from history books and other curricular materials implies that these groups are of less value, less importance, and less significance to our society than men. Literature written by women and about women's lives has not always been considered an important part of classic English literature.

And when teachers and other adults inadvertently interact more with boys than with girls, and ask girls for their opinions less frequently, they render girls invisible.

5. Keep an eye out for situations in which children are separated by gender for reasons other than toileting privacy or discussing reproduction. In education this is called *fragmentation* or *isolation*. It refers to the creation of a dichotomy that otherwise would not exist.

Examples of this in a school setting might be when staff designate a boys' line and a girls' line for walking to the art room or playground, or when, in an afterschool roller-skating program, the DJ calls all the girls to skate or compete in races against the boys.

Creating separate chapters or sections in textbooks on women's contributions and designating certain human topics as *women's issues* is commonplace. (Obviously, this happens to cultural minorities, too.) But separating instructional materials related to women from the main body of the text implies that these issues are not a part of, or are less important than, the cultural mainstream.

6. Another test for gender bias is *the sexual stereotypes test.* Ask yourself whether sex stereotypes, even *positive* ones, are being presented. When stereotypes are positive, the situation can still be sexist.

The problem with gender stereotypes is the same as the problem with racial stereotypes: gender and racial stereotypes hamper the growth of *individuals* by limiting their expectations for themselves. Meanwhile, society begins to rate one set of stereotypes as better than another. Hence, one group is perceived as being better than another. Sexism is a natural by-product of gender stereotypes. We have all learned to which group each stereotype belongs.

For example, your child's class does a history lesson on famous Americans. The men featured are George Washington, Thomas Jefferson, and Abraham Lincoln (all political leaders). The women featured are Martha Washington, Abigail Adams, and Clara Barton. Although all three are positive role models, they exemplify the attributes traditionally assigned to females. They are usually described as admirable models of supportive roles.

A selection of women who were primarily political leaders might provide a more equitable representation: Lydia Maria Child (hailed as "the first woman in the republic" by William Lloyd Garrison) was a literary genius and a household name in the early 1800s who campaigned for justice toward Native Americans, African Americans, and women; Sojourner Truth (abolitionist and suffragist), and Lucy Stone (a famous suffragist who organized the first National Women's Rights Convention).

Or, since the social context and mores for women and men of that period were very different than current ones, an analysis might be done of how these individuals exemplified role models for their times. Martha Dandridge Custis Washington was a widow of considerable wealth before George married her. As a married woman she performed her many public and private duties admirably. Abigail Smith Adams did so also, in addition to writing the often quoted plea to her husband that John and his colleagues "Remember the Ladies" in the new Constitution. Clara Barton, in addition to being "The Angel of the Battlefield," was a remarkable political organizer in the cause and funding of the American Red Cross. A feminist, and likely the first female federal civil servant, her accomplishments despite the prevailing mores are all the more extraordinary.

7. The seventh test to consider is the misogyny test. Learn to name this particular form of sexism. Once you understand its definition, you will not easily forget it.

Misogyny: *n* Hatred of women. mi-sog-y-nist *n,* mi-sog-y-nis-tic, mi-sog-y-nous *adj.*

Unfortunately, many in our culture accept an attitude of disdain for women, girls, and their characteristics. Men and boys are considered to be the norm for humans. Women and girls are the subnorm, i.e., Adam's rib.

Sometimes this can be seen in words: when the words that mean female are used as an insult, "woman," "sissy" (originally a nickname for sister), "girl," or expressions "runs like" or "throws like a girl,"

Calvin and Hobbes   by Bill Watterson

"drives like a woman!" it's misogynous and it's sexist. There are almost no negative words to insult a girl or woman that equate her with a man or a boy. Thus tomboy, which is rarely used today, is not considered to be as negative a term as sissy. (See Tip #14 on lack of parallel terms.)

Sometimes misogyny is evident in value judgments, for example, that women's issues, women's history, and women's sports have less value than men's.

8. Test language for linguistic bias, a form of sexism. Grammatical use of male gender words as inclusive of all humans (such as the generic he or mankind), is a powerful conveyor of unconscious bias.

Much has been written, of late, about language bias. Words such as *forefathers* obscure the participation of women in our history, and occupational terms like *mailman* negate the legitimacy of women working in these fields.

Studies show that children understand male-gender language to mean *male*. When asked to draw a caveman, they drew prehistoric *men*. Children who were asked to draw cave people drew *men, women, and children.*

Interestingly, and of relevance to all who encounter traditional grammarians, the use in English of male gender words as inclusive of all humans is relatively recent (c. 1553–1746), and was a change made intentionally by male grammarians.

Male gender words affect female self-esteem. This is easy to understand if you reverse male-dominant grammar to female-dominant grammar, such as changing all he's to she's, because it illustrates how important meaning is to the listener or reader. The present name for language that does not exclude people by gender (or race or religion) is *inclusive language.*

9. *Gender domination* patterns are a form of bias that can often be *visually* observed. The term refers to prerogatives that one gender group takes, or is allowed to take, over another. Observe a child's environment over time to see whether such gender patterns persist.

At this point, we cannot eliminate bias unless we look at gender patterns more carefully, identify inequities, and then work to overcome them.

When boys do not allow girls equal time on the computer or repeatedly take over the blocks or the soccer ball at lunchtime recess, that's gender domination. When nursery-school-age girls do not allow boys equal use of the play kitchen, doll corner, or dress-up clothes, that, too, is gender domination.

10. Next is the *homophobia test.* The taunts "fag," "queer," "dike," and "fairy" are examples of discrimination because of sexual orientation, real or implied. Learn to recognize and name this bias when you see or hear it.

Homophobia: *n* unreasoning fear or antipathy toward homosexuals and homosexuality.

If words, actions, or situations are homophobic, they are also sexist, because they are based on traditional sex role stereotypes.

Annie Oakley met her husband by beating him in a sharpshooting contest. After marrying, Frank Butler and his new wife took their act on the road. Frank bowed out when he realized that Annie was not only a better rider and shot, but more popular as well. He was devoted to her and worked to promote her career throughout his life.

Reproduced from the Collections of the Library of Congress.

11. Be prepared to acknowledge unconscious bias in the lack of discussion about unpleasant facts, or *unreality*. Also termed *the evaded curriculum,* these controversial topics are often glossed over in school, and discussions of discrimination, bias, prejudice, and intergroup conflict are pointedly avoided.

A child might ask "when somebody does something wrong why do the teachers always think that a boy did it?" or "why do the biggest monuments in the graveyard have mostly men's names?"

Sometimes adults avoid answering these topics, even if they are aware that a child is grappling with them, because they conflict with society's stated values of fairness and equality for all.

But saying "there's no bias here" does not help to prepare young females and males with critical thinking skills or for coping with the reality of their future lives.

12. As long as a double standard about the meaning of sexuality and sexual violence exists, explicit sexuality, in a situation where sexuality would not otherwise be considered, is sexist.

An example is the familiar depiction of members of one gender as objects. Even young children are commonly exposed to the images of scantily clad women being used to sell cars, beer, and jeans on TV. Depicting males as sex objects, however, is becoming more common, and scantily clad males also now appear in advertisements.

Explicit sexuality can be verbal, as in rating girls' attractiveness in a school hallway or by using sexual analogy to describe something as unrelated as a math problem, such as asking students to convert a woman's bust, waist, and hip measurements from inches to centimeters. It can also be visual, such as posting a calendar with pictures of nude women in a business setting.

13. Remember to ask yourself—and ask children to think about—"whose point of view is being represented?" or "who wrote the story?" In education, particularly for texts and stories, this question will help to identify *imbalance, distortion,* or *selectivity.*

Presenting only one interpretation of an issue, situation, group of people, or period can perpetuate bias. Ignoring complex or differing viewpoints can give young people an incomplete or inaccurate view of reality.

When textbooks refer to women being *"given* the vote" in 1920 but omit the challenges in that seventy–two–year struggle—the opposition funding by the liquor industry; the organizing and fundraising difficulties of many suffrage supporters across the country; and the physical abuse and lifetimes of personal sacrifice by suffrage leaders —they are imbalanced.

"My Dog Gives Them Away," Suffrage cartoon by Blanche Ames Ames, 1915. Sophia Smith Collection, Smith College.

14. Learn to hear and phase out *imbalanced word order* and *nonparallel terms* referring to females and males.

Imbalanced word order: The word order in the phrase "boys and girls" is almost always boys first, girls second. One teacher writing a math book noticed this and deliberately reversed the order for balance. The phrases "his or her," "Mr. and Mrs.," "he or she," "ladies and gentlemen" are other examples that could be reversed to neutralize this common bias.

Nonparallel terms: Words like *chivalrous* and *chaste* are used almost exclusively to describe one gender but not both. Usually, an equitable term can be substituted that might apply to either gender.

Unequal parallel terms: *Bachelor* and *spinster, housekeeper* and *butler,* are examples of parallel but unequal terms.

15. To figure out what to say or do about a sexist situation, imagine how you would respond to a similar example of racism.

For example, you might use the same type of explanation to clarify the issue to a child: "It's not really fair to hate someone because their skin is a different color or their body parts are different. Did Susie *do* something to hurt your feelings?"

Reprinted by permission of Bülbül—Gen Guracar.

two

With Concern for Boys

What you will find in this chapter:

- Tips on how to help boys avoid narrow roles

- Tips on how to help boys avoid negative roles

16. Look for a preschool or school that stresses respect for individuals as a foundation for the teaching of self-discipline.

This turns the learning of discipline toward its real goal, self-control.

Look for teachers who will take a disruptive child aside and explain that she or he is not allowed to hit, grab, yell, or tease other children or to ruin the equipment because it is not *fair* to the other children. The emphasis is not on a power struggle between teacher and child, but on having respect for and not infringing upon the rights of others.

There are many good schools that approach the teaching of discipline in a similar manner. Some Montessori* schools offer this form of discipline. Such a school is particularly helpful for boys, who often receive the message "might makes right" from society. The concept of self-discipline based on respect, as well as peaceful conflict resolution, can be introduced to children even in preschool.

* Maria Montessori (1870–1952) was the first woman graduate in Medicine from the University of Rome. She went on to apply the scientific method to the study of educational techniques, becoming world famous for the remarkable success of the educational methods that she developed and tested cross-culturally. Regarding discipline and liberty she said, "A child's liberty should have as its limit the interests of the group to which he belongs . . . We should therefore prevent a child from doing anything which may offend or hurt others, or which is impolite or unbecoming. But everything else, every act that can be useful in any way whatever, may be expressed." Dr. Montessori was nominated for the Nobel Peace Prize in 1949, 1950, and 1951.

17. Let boys cry. Offer ice if it's a physical hurt and silent sympathy, but let a boy cry. Let a boy get used to expressing his emotions. Help him to articulate frustration, loneliness, anger, shyness, sadness, and fear so that he knows and understands what he feels.

Boys have too often been cheated of their own emotions by well-intentioned parents, who are afraid that they will be "too sensitive." The crime rate, frequency of domestic violence, and sexual harassment data confirm that we do not have a problem with oversensitive males in this country. If anything, we have the opposite.

People cannot empathize with others unless they understand their own feelings. Many adults try to comfort their child by taking over the child's emotions: "You're okay" or "You're not hurt." This is confusing to a crying child who *is* feeling hurt.

We all know the familiar refrains that follow after a few moments: "Big boys don't cry," "Crybaby," "Crying is for girls," " Take it like a man," "Buck up," and finally, "That's ENOUGH now!" and "Come on now, STOP CRYING! You are making a scene!" (that is, disgracing me and yourself).

Remove a crying boy to privacy if you absolutely must, but don't override his feelings.

18. Search for and buy exciting clothes for your young son, if he enjoys them.

Boys are unnecessarily cheated out of exciting clothes.

Clothes for toddlers are bright-colored and fun, but clothes for school-age boys suddenly become drab gray, blue, red, and brown. By the time a child is old enough to do his own choosing, selections have become more standardized, offering mostly sports themes and commercial TV or movie characters.

Ordering from catalogs can help, as well as creative sewing. There are some interesting, glow-in-the-dark solar system, snap-on bug, and dinosaur T-shirts available, but the clothing industry would produce more if there were a market for clothes with braid and buttons, pleats and pin-ons, sparkle and pizzazz!

This is not to suggest that boys should be dressed like girls. The suggestion here is that boys be allowed more self-expression in the way they dress in color, texture, and variety.

19. Encourage manual dexterity and concentration in young boys. Once it becomes a goal it is easy to find many ways to do this.

Girls often arrive at school already accomplished in "small motor skills," like cutting with scissors and holding and using pencils. This may be because they have been encouraged to play with lacing, art kits, and craft projects, or to manipulate tiny doll clothes.

Boys who have often spent more time on the playground or at the sandbox playing with larger-scale toys like trucks and blocks may not have been encouraged to sit quietly and concentrate on small muscle activities. And they may not have seen males modeling such work, since many fathers do their writing away from the home, in the workplace. For some boys, the requirements of schoolwork come as a rude awakening.

Encourage young boys to participate in activities that build concentration and hand coordination. Activities that require "the three finger grip," such as inserting "LiteBrite" pegs, push pins, or manipulating small-knobbed puzzle pieces, help to build the muscles needed to control a pencil for extended periods.

20. Allow and encourage boys to dance.

Explain to children (and anyone else who will listen) about the history of men in dance and ballet. Historically, men were considered great folk dancers, performing dramatic leaps and having a formidable stage presence. This was also true of classical ballet, which men dominated from its inception in the fourteenth century. Men were the main attraction. Even the Sun King, Louis XIV of France, took lessons daily. Only in the last century, when the "toe shoe" was invented, did men cease to be the attraction that drew in the crowds. For a century, women have been the only dancers allowed to wear toe shoes, which, like stilts, give them a powerful stage presence and enable them to perform the delicate postured positions and spins. The male tradition of great leaps (and box office draw) has been revived in this century by the traditional Russian ballet dancers Rudolf Nureyev and Mikhail Baryshnikov, and such modern dance greats as Alvin Ailey, Merce Cunningham, and Paul Taylor. Today, many sports athletes enjoy dance movement and workouts as part of their physical training.

Boys who are denied a chance to dance lose a chance to learn to hear music and to synchronize their movements in time. They also miss the fun and the exercise!

Two picturebooks about boys who take dance lessons are:

Max, by Rachel Isadora, New York: Macmillan, 1976. Max finds a new way to warm up for his baseball games: he joins his sister's ballet class.

Oliver Button Is a Sissy, by Tomie de Paola, New York: Harcourt Brace, 1979. Oliver is taunted by his classmates, then later revered for his tap dancing.

21. If you hope that a young boy you care about (son, grandson, nephew) will someday grow up to be a loving, caring father, provide him with the tool of the trade, an infant doll of his own.

For children or adults who may have trouble with this idea, there is a great picturebook:

William's Doll, by Charlotte Zolotow, New York: Harper and Row, 1972. It is a story about a boy who wants a doll. His father nervously gives him other toys, like a baseball mitt, instead. He likes baseball, but continues to ask for a doll. His grandmother buys him a doll, explaining to her son (William's father) that William *should* have a doll to practice being a father.

The story of *William's Doll* is also told in song in the musical collection:

Free to Be . . . You and Me, Arista Records, 1983.
Marlo Thomas and Friends
Mailorder
J & R Music World
1-800-221-8180

If you are the one buying a doll, you may wish to consider buying an anatomically correct doll. One catalog that carries anatomically correct "newborn" dolls of five different racial appearances and with movable arms and legs is

Hand in Hand of Oxford, ME
1-800-872-9745

22. Buy and give toy cars that are small versions of family vehicles instead of race cars. Call toy companies to advise them that they are overlooking a market and request car models you would like to buy. Parents know how difficult it is to find a toy version of their family sedan, mini-van, or station wagon.

Just as thoughtful parents have become reluctant to give their sons toy guns to practice killing people, we should also consider the effect of toy race cars and (male) TV car chase scenes on the behavior of older boys and young men. *The New Read-Aloud Handbook* cites statistics that male TV characters seldom wear seat belts or glasses, yet never sustain crippling injuries from TV car crashes. When more than **twice** as many boys aged sixteen to nineteen die in cars than girls, and young men aged twenty to twenty-nine die in cars at **three times** the rate of young women of the same age, is it not time to consider the types of toy cars that boys are encouraged to play with?

Any wonder that girls don't often cross the stereotype line to buy "cars"? Unless they aspire to become race car drivers, many girls find most of the available muscle cars of marginal interest.

Matchbox: division of Tyco 1-800-367-8926
Corgi & Hot Wheels: both by Mattel 1-800-524-TOYS

23. Seek out children's books on male peacemakers, diplomats, humanitarian relief workers, and those who nurture humanity in public and private ways.

Books on the lives of William Penn, Albert Schweitzer, Linus Pauling, Nelson Mandela, and others laud the importance of such role models.

Books on men like Martin Luther King, Jr., Mahatma Gandhi, and Anwar Sadat will illustrate how courageous one must be to do this work.

24. TV and videos provide welcome entertainment for children while their parents attend to chores or other necessities, yet few adults have the time or the interest to watch what their children are watching. Parents need to know what lessons their children are absorbing, at home and in childcare settings. Make a point of watching TV programs and movies that are popular with your children and watch *with* them when possible.

This just isn't "the way things have always been." Grandparents might have received toy soldiers as children, but they weren't *shown* how to kill. Today's children see killings repeatedly on TV and can buy toys to copy this behavior. Violence is *entertainment* for younger and younger children. Today, four-year-olds watch superhero battles and teenagers have moved up to violent, bloody slasher films.

After hundreds of studies by independent researchers, experts are now warning that TV violence *does* remove inhibitions on aggression, desensitizes children to violence so that they accept it as normal and natural, and can create exaggerated fears in young children. The 1982 Surgeon General's report concluded that viewing excessive violence encourages violent behavior in children and teenagers, and has a direct, observable effect in aggressive hitting, pushing, and shoving. The American Psychological Association reiterated these findings in 1993.

What generally goes unsaid, however, is that the violence being modeled is *male* violence, male against male and male against female.

By the time the average American child finishes high school, he or she has witnessed 18,000 TV murders, the vast majority committed by men. Studies of male slasher film viewers and of films that show violence against women found that these films desensitize the viewers to such violence, both fictional and real.

If parents cannot sit through a show, maybe the children shouldn't be sitting through it either. Parents who are aware of what their children are viewing can inject valuable discussion of the values presented.

25. Not only women are feminists. Make sure children know that men can be feminists, too. Check that teachers are making this clarification. **Feminist:** *n* advocate of political, economic, and social rights for women that are equal to those of men.

Promotion of equal rights and equal opportunity is a brave and noble cause. Men who have supported feminist causes even before the term was defined at the turn of the century include Thomas Paine, Frederick Douglass, William Lloyd Garrison, Ralph Waldo Emerson, Walt Whitman, John and Melvil Dewey, Col. William F. (Buffalo Bill) Cody, and others. In this century, this wide and diverse grassroots movement for social justice has been supported by such men as Upton Sinclair, Gore Vidal, Woody Guthrie, Ed Asner, John Lennon, Howard Cosell, Alan Alda, Jesse Jackson, President Bill Clinton, and, of course, many more.

For an interesting history of men's participation in the movement for equal rights in America, consult

Against the Tide: Pro-Feminist Men in the United States 1776–1990: A Documentary History, by Michael Kimmel and Thomas Mosmiller, Boston: Beacon Press, 1992.

Ask your public library to purchase it, if it is not already in their collection. (See Tip #101)

26. Encourage (and hire) boys to do baby-sitting to gain important experience in the responsible care of young children.

Some local Red Cross chapters still offer baby-sitter certification courses, complete with CPR training. Other such courses are often offered by town recreation departments or other local community groups. Many also provide a formal certificate of completion.

This is a good job for responsible children aged twelve and up.

27. Pubescent boys need information about their changing bodies as much as pubescent girls need information about theirs. If your school does not offer a detailed program for them, be sure to read up on the subject and offer the information they need.

Boys have many concerns, although they may have been conditioned not to admit it. In our appearance-oriented culture, boys are concerned about how and when their bodies will change. Like girls, they also have embarrassing problems with the onset of physical changes (like uncontrollable erections in school or temporary swelling of breasts). They also wonder when and how they will feel attracted to girls.

Several books written for pubescent boys address some of these feelings and topics:

Boys Have Feelings Too: Growing Up Male for Boys, by Dale Carlson, New York: Atheneum Publishers, 1980. (This book is written for younger readers.)

The What's Happening to My Body? Book for Boys: A Growing Up Guide for Parents and Sons, by Lynda Madaras. New York: New Market Press, New Edition, 1987. (This book includes more about physical changes and current issues like AIDS.)

The Boy Who Wanted a Baby, by Wendy Lichtman, New York: Feminist Press, 1982. This is a story about a boy about twelve years old. Close friends of his family are about to have a baby, and he is excited and curious about sex, the wonder of new life, and what his part will be in it, someday. When the baby is born, he is named godfather!

28.   Show your son that you love him for himself, not only when he performs well or wins.

If girls/women are programmed by society to be **sex-objects,** boys/men are programmed to be **success-objects.**

The birth of a son is celebrated with the expectation that he will grow up to be a successful breadwinner, as or even more successful than his father. This is the rub of the "boys are bigger, stronger, smarter, tougher" legacy. Boys are not free to decline the challenge.

Boys are trained toward this end via competition. Winners are congratulated, encouraged, and expected to continue to the next challenge. Losers are pitied or worse, considered "unmanly," but are still expected to compete, however frustrated.

Boys are hugged and loved unconditionally until about six years of age (or eight, nine, ten, depending on the home). After that, many boys are hugged or shown love mostly when they are successful. In this way, many learn that they must earn and earn love.

Make sure a boy knows what you love about him as an individual, such as his special smile, his taste in music, or his enthusiasm for traveling.

Important titles for public and private libraries are:

 Boys Will Be Boys, Breaking the Link Between Masculinity and Violence, by Myriam Miedzian, New York: Doubleday, 1991. This book examines in detail the cultural messages that boys receive from the media and society around them.

 The Courage to Raise Good Men, by Olga Silverstein and Beth Rashbaum, New York: Viking, 1994. This book explores the importance of the mother-son relationship along with cultural expectations that it be severed; also concepts regarding male role models.

Doonesbury

BY GARRY TRUDEAU

I SPOKE TO ALEX'S TEACHER ABOUT GENDER BIAS TODAY...

A CHAT SHE WEL-COMED, NO DOUBT.

ACTUALLY, SHE WAS PRETTY COOL ABOUT IT, CONSIDERING.

I MEAN, BIAS IS A PRETTY HARD THING TO TALK ABOUT, MUCH LESS ADMIT TO...

DOES ANYONE THINK I IGNORE THE GIRLS? TEDDY?

SIGH...

three

School and Parent Interaction

What you will find in this chapter:

- What to look for at school

- What to ask for in your district

29. Avoid that old familiar phrase from our childhood, "boys and girls." It should almost never be used today except when describing something truly related to sex segregation, such as toileting or reproduction. When addressing or describing groups, use terms like *children, everyone,* or *students.*

If you hear "boys and girls" used in your child's school, your ears should prick up. It suggests that there has not been enough awareness training, and that there may be other biased practices going on, albeit inadvertently.

Calling attention to a child's gender without a valid reason creates a false dichotomy or schism. A child's gender has nothing to do with learning letters and numbers or going to the lockers to retrieve a snack. If in doubt, give the situation the racism test (see Tip #1): "Good Morning, whites and blacks . . . "

30. Remember to ask the director of a nursery school you are considering for your child what the school's policy is on gender bias. While all parents want a warm, loving, secure environment for their young child, the director's answer may make your choice between schools or teachers a very simple one!

Nursery school is often a child's first social, public experience, and it can be a very powerful one. Most preschool teachers are not certified teachers, and thus not trained in any aspects of nonsexist classroom practices. Many preschool teachers and assistants are *very* traditional in their views about the nature of girls and boys.

31. Tell teachers, school administrators, camp officials, and coaches that you are concerned about gender equity issues even before you encounter a problem.

Heading off sexism is often easier than responding to it after a sexist incident has happened. Most people do not want to promote sexism and will be more aware if they know that someone who cares is watching and is supportive of their efforts to avoid it.

For example, two children, a girl and a boy, are friends, and want to attend camp together. The parents are concerned that they will be teased. Before signing them up, the parents might question the camp about whether such teasing would be allowed. A quality camp would speak to its counselors to make sure that the camp's policy is clear: sexist teasing is unacceptable, and counselors will intervene if it occurs.

Doonesbury

BY GARRY TRUDEAU

32. Ask if the teachers in your district have had training in avoiding unconscious gender bias.

If the answer is "yes," the next questions to ask are:

- Has the school developed a policy or shared mission statement specifically about gender bias?

- Are followup observations for gender bias being conducted? (See Tip #94.)

- Who was trained? Were playground monitors, bus drivers, cafeteria monitors, specials teachers, guidance counselors, therapists, assistant teachers, and coaches trained along with regular classroom teachers?

Children don't know which adults have had education training. All adults in authority represent the school to them. A bus driver who allows sexual slurs can undo much of what a classroom teacher has worked hard to teach during the classroom day.

33. Observe a school's classrooms, lunchroom, hallways, library, playground, and buses for signs of sexism. (Don't forget to note bulletin boards, displays, and papers that come home from school!)

These can include:

- Forming separate lines of boys and girls in the hallway
- Bulletin board displays with all the girls' photos grouped together or all the boys' photos grouped together
- Displays or posters of primarily male characters
- Outings or afterschool activities for girls or for boys
- Worksheets, particularly math and science worksheets, which depict males far more often in examples or use biased language.

Some of these incidents, such as one sign-out book for boys and another one for girls, would be grounds for a lawsuit if they occurred in the workplace (see Tip #2). Yet due mostly to old habits, this type of record-keeping and crowd control is still sometimes used in schools.

Pitting the sexes against each other for spelling bees and other contests sends clear messages to children. The negative aspects of this kind of division can be clearly seen by applying Tip #1. Would a teacher today suggest, "Okay, let's get ready for a spelling contest. Jews line up on this side of the room, Christians over there?"

Similarly, if children segregate themselves in the cafeteria, on the playground, and in the classroom, this can be evidence that teachers or other staff members are not intervening often enough in instructional settings to prevent sexism. Bullying of any gender-related nature on the bus or in the hallways is a sign that there is no effective school sexual harassment policy to protect children from such verbal/physical abuse.

34. Ask administrators at your child's school about progress in replacing outdated textbooks. Ask your child's teachers how they present balanced information to students in the absence of revised texts.

We must all insist on and cherish a true representation of women, one that honors American women and women throughout history.

The contributions of Susan B. Anthony and Elizabeth Cady Stanton are every bit as important as those of Abraham Lincoln and Martin Luther King. Together they fought for and won civil rights and the vote for more citizens than anyone else in American history. Yet we have no national holiday celebrating them, and meager mention of them is made in school texts.

The "Declaration of Sentiments," a history-making document calling for women's right to vote and drafted at the 1848 Women's Rights Convention in Seneca Falls, New York, should occupy a place of honor in the National Archives along with the originals of the Declaration of Independence and the Bill of Rights. Yet the original document has been lost to us. Many Americans are not even aware of it, and know little of the seventy-two-year fight for suffrage to which many women dedicated their lives.

Perhaps today we are doing an even greater disservice to girls by telling them that they "can be anything that they want to be" without giving them the evidence of history, the necessary mentors, and proof in the world that surrounds them. Historical role models *are* there if we have the collective will to recognize and teach about them, like a self-taught founder of mathematical physics, Sophie Germaine 1776–1831. And Fanny Mendelssohn Hensel, sister of Felix, who was considered to be the more talented of the two. She wrote over five hundred compositions, but because of the social strictures of that time, she was not allowed to publish them or play for the public. Some of her pieces were published under her brother's name.

Girls are deprived of their true history, which includes the women who prevailed against formidable odds. Without such important role models, few girls have the confidence to risk bucking the entire course of history to try to beat the odds. This takes a superhuman feat of mental strength, endurance, and imagination. Clearly, the national perspective is out-of-focus for not honoring our female ancestors.

Sophie Germaine
1776–1831
Self–taught French mathematician who was a founder of mathematical physics

35. Find opportunities to explore biographies of famous women with your child.

Like anyone else, children want proof that women *can* do anything, proof that fiction does not necessarily offer. For example, every library will likely have the following biographies in the children's biography section:

Jane Addams, founder of the profession of social work, founder Hull House and winner, Nobel Peace Prize

Susan B. Anthony, suffragist and abolitionist

Dolley Madison, First Lady, hostess for Jefferson and Madison administrations, credited with magnificent entertaining and with saving the Executive Mansion's valuables from the British during the War of 1812

Maria Mitchell, astronomer, first woman elected to American Academy of Arts and Sciences, one of the first female college professors, suffragist

Lucretia Mott, abolitionist and women's suffrage leader

Betsy Ross, Philadelphia upholstery shop owner who reportedly made the nation's first flag, redesigning the stars to have five points

Many more famous women are listed at the end of this book. It is interesting that each of these prominent women was raised by Quakers and received a nonsexist education during a time when only boys were sent to school. In Quaker families (not to be confused with the celibate Shakers), girls and boys are encouraged equally. **Louisa May Alcott** and **Margaret Mead** were not Quakers, but both also attended Quaker schools.

Fanny Mendelssohn Hensel
1805–1847
German composer, some of whose work was published under the name of her brother, Felix

36. Find out whether your child's teachers are using some of the techniques that leading researchers have recommended to avoid unconscious bias and to make the classroom more encouraging for the quieter, thoughtful students (who are often girls).

Here's a checklist of ideas. Parents may also find them useful when they are in charge of groups of children:

- Do teachers use various methods to help divide the group fairly and/or involve all students? Do they for example,

  - use the class roster or names on index cards for taking turns?

  - pass out poker chips at the beginning of class, having students "pay" to talk and thereby encouraging well-considered answers?

  - have students pick up playing cards as they enter and use the cards to call on students, or to divide students into groups ("the two red jacks will be partners" or "the sixes will be the first team")?

  - divide children into teams by number of siblings, month of birthday, season of birthday, colors in clothing, counting off, alphabetical order based on mother's name, grandmother's name, great-grandmother's name?

- Do teachers use geographic mobility—do they move around and through the room so that they spend time near all students, not just the ones in the front or those who misbehave?

- Are teachers allowing enough wait time between asking a question and calling on a student to answer? A longer wait time allows children who are more thoughtful to have a chance to answer. A teacher may then choose to recognize several students, "Okay, first Mary, then Jason, then Amy."

- Are teachers breaking the class into smaller groups, actively helping children to divide themselves, and assigning roles for any cooperative learning? Are performance expectations for cooperative learning clear? Smaller groups help all students to participate and make public speaking easier.

- Are teachers intervening when students segregate or divide themselves by gender?

- Do teachers have individual meetings with some students to explain the fairness techniques they are using? Do they meet with active, talkative students who have been schooled in the traditional competitive classroom patterns as well as with those who never talk?

37. Encourage girls to take the tough classes in math and science.

Girls generally do well in math and science in elementary school, but their enrollment and scores tend to slide in middle and high school. This has important implications for college and future earnings potential (see research statistics in appendixes). As part of the "A Nation at Risk" initiative, schools have been trying to make math and science more interesting for all students and to increase competence and confidence, with very good results.

Parents can encourage their daughters by

- Expecting them to take the tough, advanced courses, rather than be overconcerned about a possible slippage in their grade point average.

- Helping them to have as many science-related experiences as possible outside of school.

It has been suggested that boys' traditional play experiences tend to give boys more familiarity with concepts that are basic ideas in later physics and chemistry classes. Girls also need to receive science kits, building kits, microscopes, and chemistry sets. Girls also need to be encouraged to repair bikes, wire electric trains, and program computers.

If a girl's friends are not interested in these kinds of hobbies, parents may have to make an extra effort to spend some time with her while she explores a science or chemistry kit. Holding a science birthday party or an astronomy slumber party mixes science and fun. Signing a girl up for a Saturday science workshop or a special camp can provide a peer group of enthusiastic friends.

38. PTA/PTOs are often looking for program suggestions. Contact the school PTA and suggest that *Shortchanging Girls, Shortchanging America* be shown at an upcoming meeting. It is a brief but convincing film by the American Association of University Women. The title says it all.

There is strength in numbers. One parent expressing concern to the school administration is very good. Twenty parents clamoring for change are much more readily heard.

If you can get your local American Association of University Women (AAUW) to lend their copy of the video to the PTA for the evening, it's a free program. Or, the video can be purchased and circulated to the school board, superintendent, other PTAs in the community, and any other individuals or groups that might be supportive. This, and the following video for parents in the AAUW series on gender bias, *Girls Can!* are also great additions to the local public library. Films like these, on gender issues and school, will help to keep the reform movement rolling.

Shortchanging Girls, Shortchanging America, an 18 min. video by the AAUW 1-800-225-9998

39. Ask to see standardized test results from your school broken down by gender. Next, propose a Gender Equity Assessment.

Evaluating standardized test scores (and enrollment in higher level math and science courses) is a vital first step to determine if and where there are problems in a particular school or district. Include an evaluation of how scores compare in the top quartile.

If further gender equity assessment is indicated, there are at least two approaches:

- A Title IX compliance review is supposed to be carried out on a continuing basis by schools that receive federal funds. Each school district is supposed to have a Title IX coordinator who is responsible for this review. This is a screening for discrimination only, not bias, but it's a start. See the definitions of *discrimination* and *bias* on page xv.

- A *Gender Equity Assessment Guide* for addressing bias issues is offered by the American Association of University Women. To use the Assessment Guide effectively, it is important to have allies within the school system and within the broader community. A spirit of collaboration, not criticism, will make this endeavor successful. Such an assessment will be more acceptable if the idea is proposed by people who work within the district, with whom administrators interact regularly.

Gender Equity Assessment Guide available from AAUW
1-800-225-9998

40. Even if your child is still in elementary school, ask if your school district has developed a sexual harassment policy. Perhaps more important, has your school talked to the children about sexual harassment and explained the school's policy?

If your school district has a policy, has there been an assembly or some other similar forum to explain what sexual harassment means and how students should respond to it? Schools that would immediately hold an assembly if there were an incident of racial or ethnic prejudice often ignore sexual harassment on a daily basis. When bra-snapping, body grabbing, and disrespectful comments are ignored, they are condoned. It is hard for students to concentrate on their studies if they are worried about being harassed.

Skits are a great format for illustrating the concepts involved. Skits, which can be performed by students for students, can be found in:

School Secrets: *Scenarios About Sexual Harassment* with a Workshop Leader's Guide, offered by AAUW 1-800-225-9998

A growing number of books and pamphlets on this topic are available. Several creative, comprehensive curriculum guides for elementary, middle, and high school classrooms are

Flirting or Hurting? A Teacher's Guide on Student-to-Student Sexual Harassment in Schools for 6th–12th Grade Students, by Nan Stein and Lisa Sjostrom, 1994, pub. by the National Education Association Professional Library, Washington, DC, 1-800-229-4200. Also available from the Wellesley College Center for Research on Women Publications Department (617) 283-2510.

Girls and Boys Getting Along: Teaching Sexual Harassment Prevention in the Elementary Classroom, by Becky Montgomery, Katia Peterson, Steve Peterson, Sue Sattel, and Susan Strauss. St. Paul, MN: Minnesota Department of Education, 1993. (Includes scripts for puppets and worksheets to color.) (612) 297-2792.

Sexual Harassment to Teenagers: It's Not Fun/It's Illegal, by Sue Sattel, St. Paul, MN: Minnesota Department of Education, 1993. (612) 297-2792.

41. Help your school district to participate in Take Our Daughters to Work Day.

This program, scheduled for the fourth Thursday in April each year, is designed to expose girls to the world of work and give them encouragement about what they can *do* rather than how they *look*. Companies and other organizations sponsor daughters, granddaughters, and nieces of employees, as well as groups of girls from schools and community organizations. During the day, girls have the chance to see what actually goes on in a workplace, to ask real questions of women and men on the job, and to try their hands at everything.

During the day, boys work on special classroom activities with guest speakers, such as men who work in nontraditional fields or interested dads.

Some schools are unwilling to take such an affirmative step. Some encourage or allow *all* students to accompany parents (or other mentors) to work that day. Others feature nonstereotypic careers for both sexes by inviting a male homemaker, nurse, kindergarten teacher, or poet to speak along with women in nonstereotypic careers. For example, one elementary school PTO created a "What's My Line?" program and invited women and men from nonstereotypic fields. What a clever, fun, and interactive way to meet an educational goal! Adjustments can be made in each district to allow for individual community goals.

To purchase a Take Our Daughters to Work organizational packet, which includes guidelines for offices as well as for the school district and parents, call the Ms. Foundation, New York, NY (212) 742-2300.

42. If it looks as though changes in a school district will not occur in time to help your daughter, particularly one who is struggling academically or with self-esteem issues, you might consider single–gender schooling.*

In addition to the tips in this book and other strategies adults might devise in working with their school system, there is the possibility of single-gender education for girls.

When educators recommend that girls be educated in single-gender schools, they sometimes say "girls are different," "that classrooms should provide for their needs," and that, for the average girl, "several years in a single-sex setting statistically predicts greater future achievement." It is important for parents to understand that they are referring to *cultural* not *biological* differences. What some educators are suggesting is that girls are often not highly valued in a co-ed setting.

Specifically why single-gender schooling results in greater achieve-ment levels for girls is not well studied because the education of girls has never been well studied. Some public schools, in an effort to develop methods that will help encourage girls in math and science, have initiated voluntary single-sex classes. For the most part, these

---

*Note: This advice does not necessarily apply to boys. See sections on single–gender schooling for boys: "The Jury Is Still Out" and "Lost in the Past" in *Failing at Fairness*.

are considered *temporary* experiments, designed to develop techniques and methods that can later be used to encourage all students in coed classrooms.

The main advantages of single–gender schools for girls appear to be that:

- a girl is not penalized for being female in teacher-student interactions
- a girl sees girls modeling all roles—class president, team captains, valedictorian
- a girl is less likely to experience conflict between her academic and social relationships with boys or to face sexual harassment

A particular single-gender school may or may not offer additional advantages:

- an affirmative curriculum and avoidance of linguistic bias
- an inclusive program that assures a child equal access to equipment and classroom participation (single-gender schools that are modeled exclusively on the competitive model of nineteenth-century boys' schools may not bring out the full potential of a quiet, thoughtful child of either sex)

 The National Coalition of Girls' Schools
Concord, MA (508) 287-4485

Essential titles for public and school libraries are

 Failing at Fairness: How America's Schools Cheat Girls, by Myra and David Sadker (professors, American University), New York: Charles Scribner's Sons Publishers, 1994, 347 pages. This comprehensive study also includes a chapter on "The Miseducation of Boys."

 The AAUW Report: How Schools Shortchange Girls, 128 pages;
Hostile Hallways: The AAUW Survey on Sexual Harassment in America's Schools, 28 pages.
Both published by The American Association of University Women, Wash., DC 1-800-225-9998

 SchoolGirls: Young Women, Self-Esteem, and the Confidence Gap, by Peggy Orenstein (with the AAUW), New York: Doubleday, 1994, 277 pages. This book contains interviews with adolescent girls and some reporting on gender-equal classrooms.

Other resources:

 The Center for Research on Women at Wellesley College
Wellesley, MA
(617) 283-2500
Ask for information about the Seeking Educational Equity
and Diversity (S.E.E.D.) Project.

 The Marymount Institute for the Education of Women
and Girls
Tarrytown, NY
(914) 332-4917
Dr. Ellen Silber, Director. Subscribe to *Equity: Newsletter for
the Education of Women and Girls.*

 Consortium for Educational Equity
Rutgers University, Kilmer Campus
New Brunswick, NJ
(908) 445-2071

 EQUALS, Lawrence Hall of Science
University of California at Berkeley
(510) 642-1823
programs designed to increase participation of young
women and minorities in science, math, and computing

The Equity Institute
Bethesda, MD
(301) 654-2904
American women in science videos, books, and teaching
guides geared toward elementary grades

Minnesota State Department of Education
Office of Gender Equity
St. Paul, MN
(612) 297-2792

Women's Action Alliance
New York, NY
(212) 532-8330
provides resources and training for girls in computer
equity

The Arthur and Elizabeth Schlesinger Library on the
History of Women in America at Radcliffe College
Cambridge, MA
(617) 495-8647
Radcliffe's collection is the closest we have to a National
Collection of information about women's history and
issues. Significant documents have been donated to its

archives relating to women's suffrage, political participation, social history, and a range of other topics. The librarians at the reference desk may be of help in guiding the reader toward sources of information on particular subjects.

National Women's History Project
Windsor, CA
(707) 838-6000
all kinds of materials for home and school, plus teacher training, free catalog

Organization for Equal Education of the Sexes, Inc.
Blue Hill, ME
(207) 374-2489
posters of famous women

Liz, break it to her gently, ruffles and lace are not the real me.

Reprinted by permission of Bülbül—Gen Guracar.

four

The Environment at Home

What you will find in this chapter:

- Tips for parents on encouraging self-esteem in their daughters

- Tips for fathers and daughters

- Purchasing power

43. Greeting cards can be great perpetuators of sex-stereotyping, but if you look around a little, you can usually find wonderful cards that don't impose a gender expectation on their recipients.

Start right at the beginning with congratulatory birth cards!

A new baby is a wondrous miracle!
Joyous congratulations!

or:

A child is one of life's greatest riches.
Congratulations on making a bundle!

44. Make an extra effort to allow children to be exposed to women in business. If you are simply choosing a name out of the yellow pages, why not utilize the services of female professionals?

pediatricians

dentists

orthodontists

allergists

printers

plumbers

painters

architects

Also, for the same reason, male nurturers:

tutors

home health aides

community art, music, theatre, and dance teachers

45. The next time you are faced with a bored child, imagine for a second that the child is of the opposite sex (i.e., a son instead of a daughter). You will instantly think of at least three activities the child has not been introduced to yet!

46. There are wonderful new rhymes available to substitute for old-fashioned sexist ones. Don't hesitate to use them with children!

Many adults are well aware that many old-fashioned classics, a product of their times, are often sexist.

Sugar and spice and everything nice . . .

Snakes and snails and puppy dog tails . . .

What many may not realize is that these rhymes have already changed and evolved over the years. Sometimes, even parents may not know what the words mean well enough to explain them to children—who do ask!

For example, how many parents realize that "Ring around the Rosie" may very well be a children's play burial ritual about the Great Plague? How many parents know that "Little Miss Muffet" was the daughter of Thomas Muffet, a spider expert who administered to her the common cold remedy of two hundred years ago, eating mashed spiders. Of course she ran away! (See *Amazing Spiders,* by Alexandra Parsons. New York: Alfred Knopf, 1990.) And, (Little) Jumping Joan was a term for "a lady of little reputation."

Adults who would like to know more about what these nursery rhymes mean may wish to consult:

The Oxford Dictionary of Nursery Rhymes, by Iona and Peter Opie, Oxford: Oxford University Press, 1983.

Parents and teachers know that hearing rhyming verse is very important for young children. It sharpens their listening skills for letter sounds in preparation for reading and writing. What to do?

There are many wonderful, memorable bedtime poetry collections either to buy or to borrow from the library. You may find that your children's favorites become new family classics. There is also *Father Gander's Nursery Rhymes,* a painless new version that generally alters only a word or two of the well-known rhymes or simply adds an additional verse for balance.

Father Gander's Nursery Rhymes,
by Douglas Larche, Santa Barbara, CA: Advocacy Press, 1985.

Peter, Peter, Pumpkin Eater,
Had a wife and wished to keep her,
Treated her with fair respect,
She stayed with him and hugged his neck!

47. When buying gifts for children, try not to fall into the trap of buying girls' toys and boys' toys, unless a child has specifically asked for them.

If ever there was any question about whether our society has changed its attitudes toward sexual stereotypes, one look at the arsenal for boys and the pink and mauve doll aisle in most toy stores reveals that we are preparing children for the same old roles. Some toy stores even label the aisles girls and boys, but even if they don't, everyone knows which categories each toy belongs to.

Try to select science, astronomy, and nature kits, books, art equipment, music tapes or instruments, sports or camping equipment, magic kits, games (nonsexist, of course) and cards, puzzles, computer software, or some of the newer history sets like hieroglyphics code kits. There is no shortage of fun and educational toys that do not perpetuate the old role models.

48. If you only have a few minutes in the library to choose books (as many harried parents do) and don't have time to read the whole text, check the date of the copyright. You will be less likely to bring home a sexist book if you choose a post–1970 book.

Be a little wary of children's books written before the 1970s. Before the enlightenment of the feminist movement, texts tended to promote very narrow images of women. A copyright date is certainly no guarantee—sexist books continue to be produced today—but if you are pressed for time choosing a book by a female author can be an additional quick sorting method, although by *no* means a guarantee: there are many wonderful children's books by gifted male authors, and very sexist ones by female authors.

Since the late 1970s, children's books have been reviewed for multicultural content. As a result, it is difficult to find current bibliographies that deal selectively with gender roles. A bibliography of children's books has been included in the appendixes. (See also Tip #96.)

49. Think of the types of things that you might say in greeting a boy, and try to greet girls in a similar way.

Try to avoid commenting on young girls' clothes or appearance when you greet them. You wouldn't be likely to remark on a boy's appearance. Clearly, girls learn early that they are judged on their physical appearance, especially when people repeatedly comment on how they look instead of what they do and say.

50. One way of dealing with classic children's literature which, though sexist, finds its way into every home, is to ask children, "How do you think a similar situation could be handled today?"

We all know that Cinderella should have moved out and gotten her own apartment. But do young children know? Help children to understand that in today's society there are ways to overcome some of the problems depicted in those classic plots. When the problem to surmount is evil magic, this probably won't work, but in other plots children can be challenged to think how the situation might be saved without a princely rescue. How might Rapunzel have escaped from that tower on her own? Practice how children *should* answer a stranger they might meet like the wolf in *Little Red Riding Hood*.

51. Keep rugged play in mind when you shop for both girls' and boys' clothes.

Girls' clothing is invariably pink or pastel-colored. As a result it soils easily, provoking reprimands to girls about ruining or dirtying their clothes.

Similarly, girls' clothing (so labeled in stores and catalogs, and sized and buttoned differently from boys' clothing) offers little knee protection. Where boys wear pants that are often reinforced in the knees, girls are more likely to wear knitted leggings (or, dresses with *no* leg protection). Any girl who rides a bike, runs, or climbs risks falling and suffering hamburger knees. Any kid subjected to those odds is not going to take the risk of active play as often. Worse, at her young age she may conclude that boys must really be tougher, not realizing that clothes make the man!

There are some great dark-colored clothes for girls that do offer enough protection for active play. Many are beautifully decorated, if that is important to your child. Clothes that encourage more active play are not hard to find once you know what to look for! Catalogs can make the job of purchasing unisex jeans or sweats easier if girls are sensitive about entering the boys' department of a store.

52. Try to avoid commercial television for children. Instead tape TV shows and zip through the commercials, or rely instead on public television and videos.

Commercial TV characters are generally limited, and plots stereotypic. Commercials, especially those targeted toward children, are worse! There is little regulation of violence or commercials on children's television because politicians are afraid of network reprisals come reelection time.

If your children really like some of the commercial shows, try to watch a few of them to evaluate the content. Even *Power Rangers,* which has strong female characters, occasionally has them saying things like, "I can only balance shopping bags." TV can provide welcome entertainment and even educational content, but adults should find time to watch what their children are watching and see what lessons they are absorbing.

Videos such as *Beauty and the Beast, Pippi Longstocking, She–Ra Princess, Mary Poppins, Little Women, Alice in Wonderland, Friendly Persuasion,* and *The Wizard of Oz* offer strong female characters and some positive male role models. Both sexes will watch them. Since young children ask for the same videos over and over again, you may wish to buy the ones that present the best role models.

For parents without a lot of time to shop there is a mail-order business that will mail a free video catalog:

 Critic's Choice Video
1-800-367-7765

53. If your child's wish list for birthdays or holidays seems uninspired (*another* Barbie—when there are four Barbies lying on the floor of the closet—or *another* model car), try imagining for a few minutes that your girl is a boy or your boy a girl. You will certainly think of a gift that is mind-expanding and appropriate—and one that your child doesn't already own!

At last!

Ms. Potato Head

Look for this liberated spud

at your local store

or write: Parker Sisters
42 Artichoke Way
Castroville, CA

54. The next time you help your child clean her or his room, make a stack of those books that show female protagonists and another of those that depict male protagonists. Does this exercise suggest the need for a more equitable balance?

Pay attention to animal and cartoon characters, who are usually assigned a gender, and to whether the characters represent gender stereotypes. Of the female protagonists, how many can be considered adventurous compared to how many are working out a social or emotional problem?

This exercise can also be tried in your child's classroom, where books are often read aloud by teachers, lent for home use, or listed as reading assignments.

It can also be done at home with toys, often at a glance. Does your child own primarily male-stereotyped toys, female-stereotyped toys?

55. Visualize your child as being of the opposite sex and then monitor your own reactions as you encounter your child.

For example, the assumption that boys can't control themselves, need to move around more, are more active, and fidget more leads to differences in the way the two sexes are disciplined.

When a boy does something physically inappropriate, like jumping on a couch, he is likely to be allowed to continue for a few seconds longer than a girl would be before being reprimanded. This has been documented in the classroom, where boys who yell out the answer are allowed to do so, while girls are reprimanded for the same behavior. Girls and boys both notice these subtleties, if unconsciously, and rise to adult expectations.

Teachers are being advised to try harder *not* to do this. Families are advised to hold the same standards of self-control for both genders.

As you try this, are you a little more tolerant of a girl running through the mall if you picture her as your son? Are you a little less tolerant of a boy roaring through the store if you picture him as your daughter?

56. Although postal issues change often, there are almost always some stamps available that depict famous women. Buy them and make sure your children have opportunities to use them.

The U.S. Postal Service is one of our most important national institutions to honor American women. Post office literature and even the stamps themselves often describe the contributions of the individual depicted. Girls receive some comfort and positive role modeling when they see American institutions honoring the image of a woman. Boys gain perspective and respect.

It is best if you can buy enough of an issue so that the whole family can use them routinely. The most commonly used first-class stamps rarely depict a woman, however. You may need to buy sheets of, for example, the "Legends of the West" series, and tear out the Annie Oakley and Sacagawea stamps to give children for their mail. (Use the remainder of the cow*boy* stamps to mail the bills.)

57. If you are having trouble locating great reading material that depicts strong female characters, try turning off the lights and making up an epic bedtime story about a strong girl (or daughter). You'll have a chance to include risk-taking, a little safety planning, and, of course, triumph at the end!

If you have trouble getting started, take an adventure story like Robin Hood, Tom Sawyer, or Jack and the Beanstalk and substitute.

58. When you watch commercial TV with children, make a game out of watching the commercials. Ask them to guess what is being sold and to envision the sex roles reversed.

Envision a man dancing around the bathroom in an apron, smiling, nuzzling the towels and singing about how much he loves using his particular fabric softener. It won't be long until your children begin to notice and point out sexual stereotypes on their own.

59. Get some Susan B. Anthony dollar coins from your bank and keep them on hand so that you can use them frequently with children.

The only U.S. currency currently honoring an American woman is the Susan B. Anthony dollar. Unfortunately, the coin is unpopular because of its quarterlike size, and thus is not commonly circulated.

It almost makes more of an impression, however, if it is used for special purposes, such as tooth fairy or birthday money, or even for allowance or payment for special jobs.

60. Fathers, buy your daughter a subscription to a science, mechanics, or computer magazine, such as *Omni, Popular Science, National Geographic.* The subscription should be in her own name. Do not expect that she won't like mechanics, boat racing, automotive history, or trains. If she does these things with you, chances are that she will!

61. It is very important for fathers, as well as mothers, to show genuine interest in a daughter's sporting events, to attend them, and to support equal funding and billing of girls' sports teams.

62. Attribute a girl's success to her *abilities,* not to luck, circumstance, hard work, or effort.

It has been suggested by researchers that girls pick up on and internalize the attitudes of adults that boys are really the smart ones—they just don't try. (See research summaries in appendix B.)

Thus, when boys achieve, they attribute their success to ability ("I'm pretty good at algebra"). If they fail they attribute it to lack of effort, not stupidity ("I can't believe it! I must have studied the wrong stuff. I should have gotten a better grade than this").

When girls succeed, they attribute their success to effort ("I really worked on this"). If they fail, they attribute it to lack of ability ("I'm just not smart enough in algebra").

Internalizing success and externalizing failure (the male model) fortifies the individual to approach challenging tasks confidently and to persevere in the face of difficulty, which lead to further achievement and success.

Children who attribute success to effort and failure to lack of ability (the female model) have learned not to persist when they encounter difficulty. They have learned to think, "I can't."

63. Consider providing some single-sex activities for a daughter, such as Girl Scouts, Girls, Inc., or an all-girl computer or sports camp.

In a single-gender setting, girls are more likely to have a chance at leadership roles, and to get the hands-on experience of being involved in every facet of an activity. In a mixed group, girls often end up as spectators.

64. Allow girls excessive amounts of time to play around with the home computer or lobby the school for access to the school's equipment so that girls can spend lots of extra time on it. Encourage girls to dominate the machinery and to experiment.

Computer literature and software illustrations have been shown to be clearly oriented toward males. Boys and men are socialized to want equipment that is bigger, faster, and cooler than the next guy's. Also, boys and men are socialized to dominate or be dominated. Computers are often balky and uncooperative. Boys who have been socialized to believe that equipment is theirs to dominate will spend inordinate amounts of time and effort to make the machine obey them.

Girls tend to give up far more easily. They are typically more interested in how the computer can be useful in accomplishing a task and lose interest when it is not. These differences are important for parents encouraging their children on computers to realize and compensate for as necessary.

Children of both genders learn to love the computer through playing games, but video games such as *Nintendo* have been documented as being both violent and unappealing to many girls. They are also expensive. Parents may want to consider investing in a home computer for which there are many new adventure games instead. Both genders enjoy these games, like "Amazon Trail," which offer real intellectual challenges—going on adventures, solving mysteries, and decoding puzzles. Best of all, children learn transferable computer skills that they will need someday in their adult lives.

Also, parents who are encouraging daughters to use the computer information superhighway should be aware that it can sometimes be hostile to female users. Computers are perceived by some male users as a male domain. Because the system is anonymous, young women who log on with an obvious female name have reportedly received sexual messages. Parents may need to be prepared to help a daughter deal with this.

U.S. Navy Admiral Grace Hopper
1906–1991
Inventor of COBOL computer language (and originator of the phrase "there's a bug in it!")

Courtesy of the Department of Defense.

Lady Ada Lovelace
1815–1852
Inventor of programming for the first computer

65. Listen to a daughter carefully. Parents should know that girls' self-esteem problems appear around age twelve (fifth grade to middle school). At ages eight, nine, and ten they are full of life and confidence. At twelve, when their bodies begin to change into women's bodies, there is a tendency (for some more than others) to retreat inside themselves, to become very unsure and never fully regain that former confidence.

Girls are socialized to be good, nice, and perfect, messages that certainly are not directed toward boys after age five! By the time they reach their teenage years, they have internalized these messages. It's a pretty hard standard to live up to, especially because the culture seems to reward its opposite, aggressive competition and risk taking at school, in sports, and in business. Girls need support. It's not just hormones.

Parents should also know that some girls who appear to be at risk of developing anorexia and bulimia are good, high-achieving students whom parents might not suspect of having self-esteem problems. In many instances, it is high-achieving white girls who are determined to achieve the flat stomachs and lithe bodies modeled in so many magazines, catalogs, and TV, and who succumb to diet messages. They can be very secretive about their goals and methods. This is why it is so important to listen carefully to daughters and to question unrealistic beauty standards openly. (See Tip #92.)

For more information on this developmental age, each of the following books discusses adolescent girls' perceptions of issues they face:

Meeting at the Crossroads: Women's Psychology and Girls' Development, by Lyn Mikel Brown and Carol Gilligan, Cambridge, MA: Harvard University Press, 1992, 258 pages.

Reviving Ophelia: Saving the Selves of Adolescent Girls, by Mary Pipher, New York: Grosset/Putnam, 1994, 293 pages.

SchoolGirls: Young Women, Self-Esteem, and the Confidence Gap, by Peggy Orenstein (with the AAUW), New York: Doubleday, 1994, 277 pages.

forthcoming in fall 1995:

Between Voice and Silence: Women and Girls, Race and Relationships, by Jill McLean Taylor, Carol Gilligan, and Amy M. Sullivan, Cambridge: Harvard University Press.

Excellent resources on parent-daughter relationships:

 The Difference: Growing up Female in America, by Judy Mann, New York: Warner Books, 1994, 295 pages.

 How to Father a Successful Daughter, by Nicky Marone, New York: Fawcett Crest, 1987, 217 pages.

 Mother-Daughter Revolution: From Good Girls to Great Women, by Elizabeth Debold, Marie Wilson, and Idelisse Malave, New York: Bantam Books, 1994, 299 pages.

Some sources for nonsexist materials:

 Audio Tapes/CD's:
Free to Be . . . a Family, A & M Records, 1988.
Free to Be . . . You and Me, Arista Records, 1983.
Marlo Thomas and Friends
(Mel Brooks, Harry Belafonte, Diana Ross, Carol Channing, Dick Cavett . . .)
Mailorder
J & R Music World
1-800-221-8180

Picture book biographies, *Great Women* cards, coloring
books and paper placemats to color, as well as adult
reference books are also available from:
National Women's History Project, Windsor, CA.
For a free catalog call: (707) 838-6000

 A wonderful series of card games played like Rummy or
Go-Fish is called *Great Women* biographical card games.
The five games are entitled: Foremothers, Founders and
Firsts, Poets and Writers, Composers, and Athletes, manu-
factured by Aristoplay Ltd., Ann Arbor, MI.
For a distributor or a catalog call: 1-800-634-7738

 A mail order source for nonsexist children's and parenting
books is Chinaberry Book Service, Spring Valley, CA
1-800-776-2242

"I wonder why people say 'Amen' instead of 'Awomen'?"
"I know! Because they sing hymns, not hers!"

five

Sexist Language

What you will find in this chapter:

- Dos and don'ts in word choices

- Confidence builders

66. If you teach children about avoiding male-dominant word choices, they will amaze you with their perceptiveness. Children are very adept at questioning vocabulary that adults assimilated long ago but which is new and fresh to them!

Many of us have already learned to use *police officer, letter carrier,* and *flight attendant* for the words *policeman, mailman,* and *stewardess.* The harder ones to ferret out and replace, such as a grandfather clause or mastering a skill, require continued diligence. (See appendix A for a guide to Nonbiased, Inclusive Language.)

For example, the principal sends home a note describing what steps should be taken in the event of an unforeseen school closing. As you are busy reading the note to try to figure out which bus your child should board, your child asks, "Why does the letter say natural or *man-made* disaster?" These phrases are new to children and they examine every word.

It may take a few extra minutes to come up with a substitute. The suggested substitutions, *synthetic* and *artificial,* don't really apply in this case. Within a few minutes you'll come up with something like *human-engineered* or *human-error.* Meanwhile, it's been a great intellectual exercise for you and your child!

67. Use the pronoun "it" when referring to an animal if you are not absolutely sure of its sex. This includes dinosaurs!

There is a tendency to assign a sex to animals even if we don't know what sex they are, and the assigned gender is usually male. Animals and fictional animal characters, especially those that are predatory, strong, and reptilian, are called "he" even if they could be "she." When you are unsure, the accurate, scientific term is "it."

A common observation of a wild animal would be, "Oh! Look at that turtle! He's swimming near that log!" It is uncommon to hear, "Oh! Look at that turtle! She's swimming near that log!"

The danger of this practice is that kids come to think that there are *no* female Tyrannosaurus Rexes, King snakes, and sharks (see Tips #4 and #8). It also reinforces the idea that female is associated only with soft, furry, mammalian creatures such as bunnies, lambs, and kittens.

68. Help girls to not put themselves down and to avoid learned helplessness.

Girls learn that if they quit or say that they aren't able to do something, an adult might come along and do it for them. This has been documented in classrooms, where teachers force a boy to struggle with a problem but help a girl by showing her the solution. What this teaches girls is called *learned helplessness;* it saps their confidence in their own ability to solve problems.

You can help by not allowing girls to profess incompetence in areas where they do need to become proficient. Make it a rule not to allow "I'm not good at . . . ," "I can't do it," and "I don't know hooooooow . . . ." Let girls know that you will only accept, "I can't do it, *yet.*"

69. We must retrain ourselves to say "women and men" to reflect—for children and ourselves—what is accurate. Also, the common phrase "women and other minorities" is so erroneous it needs correcting wherever you encounter it.

Women are *not* a minority group! Women are the MAJORITY, comprising between 51 and 53 percent of the population, depending on who is doing the counting. The average world citizen is most likely a woman of color. (See Tip #14 on word order.)

70. Use sports metaphors at home with girls.

This should be considered a survival strategy. What is being suggested is not that our society needs to be more competitive and sports-oriented, but rather, that our society is already very sports-oriented, and that girls in particular may need to be able to use these metaphors for effective communication. Girls and boys who don't already hear enough of this will find it useful later on, either in sports or in communication with adults who have played on teams and value sports highly.

Let's level the playing field.

He dropped the ball.

We've scheduled a kick-off meeting.

We've got to take some time-out.

I'm not going to sit on the sidelines and watch you.

We've got to start the ball rolling.

It's time to fall back and punt.

Next we'll tackle . . .

71. When referring to the subject of having children, say to a girl, as you would to a boy, "Someday, when you grow up, *if you decide that you want to* be a parent . . . " (not "Someday, when you're a Mommy . . . ").

Adults should avoid emphasizing girls' ability to bear children, lest girls come to think that it is the *only* thing of importance that they will do in their lives.

This has the additional advantage of preparing girls to feel worthwhile even if they later do not have children for physical or other reasons.

72. For females, use Ms. or no title.

Aside from marital status/privacy issues, *Mrs.* is really an abbreviation for *mistress of* and is only correctly used with a man's name (Mrs. Donald Smith).

If you find yourself in an awkward situation, explain what *Mrs.* really means. Other people will get it.

Does this mean that you should throw away the family stationery? No, but the next time you order some or have return address labels or a rubber stamp made, take this issue of titles into account.

73. Be careful about using words and expressions that convey a negative stereotype of women's protests or self-assertion.

These terms are almost exclusively reserved for females:

nagging	fishwife
scolding	shrew
sassy	on the rag
harping	henpeck
fuss	bitch or bitchy

These words help to perpetuate the stereotypes that men who are considered powerful protest, chew-out, or take action. But the words henpeck, bitch, or harp describe women in similar situations. Also, it is culturally suggested to boys that, should they complain, they are more likely to receive ridicule than rescue or help, since they are supposed to be the rescuers.

74. Teach girls to use *"would* you?" and *"will* you?" instead of *"could* you?" and *"can* you?" which are often gender-segregated (and incorrect)."Would you"/"will you" conveys *intent,* but "could you"/"can you" conveys only *ability to.*

One danger of allowing children to segregate themselves by sex is that each group develops different behavior codes and speech patterns. This makes future communication and understanding between the sexes much more difficult when they reach adulthood.

The can/will and could/would word choices, astutely pointed out in John Gray's popular *Men Are from Mars, Women Are from Venus,* are a good example. Women tend to use *"could* you do this for me?" or *"can* you do this?" Men tend to use *"would* you do this for me?" or *"will* you do this?" Furthermore, men are sometimes *insulted* if the words "can" and "could" are directed toward them, because it implies that the questioner thinks they *may not be capable* of doing the requested action.

A wife might ask her husband, *"Can* you wash the porch floor?" The husband replies, "Yes."

She means "Can you fit the task into your schedule, and if so, will you do it?" When he says, "Yes," she thinks he has answered yes to her question and that the porch floor will be washed.

But he heard the question as "Are you *capable* of washing the floor?" He answers, "Yes." What he means is that he is capable of washing the floor but feels irritated about having his ability questioned and doesn't necessarily feel that he has promised to do the task.

Some have suggested that women consider *could/can* to be the more polite phrasing, and that those who are in a subservient position (cross-culturally) habitually make more polite word choices. Others have suggested that the traditional division of labor, in which women, "whose work is never done," respond to the perceived needs of others, causes them to think of such requests in terms of scheduling. Men, "who work from sun to sun" and are socialized to consider public image and performance, have learned to make decisions about specifically stated commands or requests.

Essentially, however, cultural gender division is the culprit, and the potential for misunderstandings at the office, as well as at home, is obvious. Teach girls to use *will* and *would* with everyone unless they are referring to a true capability issue.

75. Help girls to avoid qualifiers and tag questions when they speak.

At home, in your Scout troop, or at Sunday school, anywhere that you are responsible for girls, show them that you will not accept qualifiers that indicate they aren't confident in their answers or thinking. Like self-put-downs (see Tip #68) qualifiers can undermine the power of what they say.

"I'm not sure, but . . . "

"You probably aren't looking for this but . . . "

"I'm a little uncertain . . . "

"I guess . . . "

"Kind of . . . "

Call attention to questions or inflections like

"Okay?"

"Is it . . . ?"

"Isn't it . . . ?"

Again, it has been suggested that these speech patterns develop because of differences in social status. Women (and other cultures such as the Japanese) tend to perceive these qualifiers as more polite.

Studies show that men perceive women more favorably if they use them, reinforcing the behavior.

Boys in American culture learn early that these qualifiers indicate hesitation and weakness, and they tend not to use them, to mask their uncertainty.

Teaching girls to talk more like boys is a survival skill and can be perceived as androcentric, but it is also important for both girls and boys to understand how to communicate effectively with many different people under many different circumstances.

76. You may have to update your dictionaries. Check for definitions that relate to sexism.

Spunky children are likely to look up for themselves the words used in our culture to discuss gender rights: *feminism, sexism, misogyny,* and *homophobia.* But word definitions continue to evolve, and it is the job of the dictionary compilers to reflect current thinking on the meaning of a word accurately. Dictionaries reflect the time in which (and those by whom) they were compiled.

A 1979 Webster's definition of **fem' i nism,** *n.* . . . . 1. (a) the *theory* that women should have political, economic, and social rights equal to those of men; (b) the movement to win such rights for women. 2. feminine qualities. (Rare.) (emphasis added).

A 1993 Webster's definition of **fem' i nism,** *n.* . . . . 1. (a) the *doctrine* that women should have political, economic, and social rights equal to those of men; (b) the movement to win such rights for women. 2. feminine qualities. (Rare.) (emphasis added).

77. Encourage your PTA or other community organizations to donate inclusive language reference guides to school libraries and all classrooms.

A MUST for every public and school library is a reference guide to nondiscriminatory language. One such volume is:

The Dictionary of Bias-Free Usage: A Guide to Nondiscriminatory Language, by Rosalie Maggio, Oryx Press, 1991, 293 pages.

The list of nonsexist words in Appendix A was taken from a one-page brochure, *A Practical Guide to NonSexist Language,* and is reprinted with permission. The *Practical Guide* is produced by a member of the St. Louis chapter of the National Organization for Women (NOW). Such a guide would be an effective and very low cost PTA/PTO contribution to *every* classroom in a school district, especially if a trip to the school library to consult a reference volume is inconvenient for both teachers and students.

A Practical Guide to NonSexist Language, St. Louis County NOW, Kirkwood, MO
(314) 822-0711

78. Resist the urge to determine the gender of a baby you do not know before speaking. Instead, try to avoid using the pronouns that require it.

Because we think we need to determine the gender of a person before we speak about them, we try to ascertain the gender of unfamiliar adults and children. This is necessitated by our language's pronouns (see Tip #80). Unfortunately, a lot of sex-stereotyping tends to go along with these gender distinctions.

It is easier to avoid gender bias altogether if we don't make a determination about gender. This is easily practiced with strangers whom we encounter in situations that do not require personal pronouns.

In a grocery checkout line you might say, "How old is *your baby?*" (instead of "How old is *she?*").

For more information on gendered speech and communication patterns attributed to learned experience in childhood, consult the books listed here by Deborah Tannen, professor of Linguistics at Georgetown University:

 You Just Don't Understand: Men and Women in Conversation. New York: Ballantine Books, 1990.

 Talking from 9 to 5: How Women's and Men's Conversational Styles Affect Who Gets Heard, Who Gets Credit, and What Gets Done at Work. New York: William Morrow, 1994.

Doonesbury

BY GARRY TRUDEAU

six

Helping Kids Cope

What you will find in this chapter:

- Tips on helping children to negotiate social customs

- Help in counteracting the pressures of stereotypes

- How kids should deal with sexual harassment

79. Never allow adults or other children to tease a child about girlfriends, boyfriends, or dating.

Just as adults must be allowed to work together without the supposition of sexual involvement, children of every age group must be allowed the freedom to associate, work together, and play together without fear of such teasing.

80. The English language requires that we know which sex a particular person belongs to. Explain this to young children so that they will understand *why* people will want to know whether they are girls or boys.

Our language, like all the Romance languages, developed from Latin and many other languages, requires that we determine a person's gender.

Since it is considered impolite to refer to a person as "it," one must know a person's sex in order to use the pronouns *he, she, his, hers, him,* and *her* correctly. (It is also considered unacceptable to walk around naked.) The only way to know which English pronouns to use is by agreed-upon male and female dress codes.

81. Explain to children that pink for girls and blue for boys is fashion, and, like any other style, it comes and goes. But it is sexist. Try not to buy pink or blue gender-specific wrapping paper, greeting cards, clothes, or toys.

There are plenty of wonderful items available that don't perpetuate out-dated stereotypes.

Before 1920, children under the age of six generally wore white. After approximately age six, children were dressed like miniature adults. In the 1920s, a new interest in differentiating the sexes at an earlier age developed. It became fashionable for boys' color to be pink (a more vibrant color) and girls' to be blue (a more placid, serene color). The present fashion (pink for girls, blue for boys) came about only in the late 1930s.

Having explained shifting fashion to a child, and why you don't buy items you don't approve of, you may find that the child still wants to purchase a stereotyped item. Suggest that an older child make the purchase with her or his own money; if it seems important to give in to a younger child, at least the message has registered at the conscious level.

82. One way to soften the blow of society's gender stereotyping for young children is to choose words that convey these standards as the conventions of a particular time and/or place.

Phrases like

- "In our culture we . . . "
- "Today it is the custom to . . . "
- "It is the fashion now to . . . "
- "Years ago people thought that . . . but now we think . . . "
- "When grandma was a child people used . . . Now we use . . . I wonder what we might be using when you are grown-up?"

Thus, a small boy who wants long fingernails can be assured that in China, it once was the fashion for affluent men to grow long fingernails. Or that men once wore wigs, curls, ruffles, and silk stockings. Or that in the sixteenth century, *only* men wore high heels. Or that women in history have led men into battle. Or that in the agrarian society before the Industrial Revolution, men were mostly at home on family  farms and participated more in the raising of their children.

This helps to reassure a child that her or his sex is not in jeopardy due to an interest, ability, or fashion.

83. Explain to children what sexism is.

The direct approach is the most effective. When we teach children about racism, we teach them to recognize overt discrimination: "That drinking fountain is only for _____ ." Today we must teach children to recognize sexism: "That toy (sport, behavior, activity) is only for _____ ."

A great book for children who have already been out in the world a bit is:

 X: A Fabulous Child's Story, by Lois Gould, New York: Daughters Publishing Co., 1978 or in *Stories for Free Children,* edited by Letty Cottin Pogrebin, New York: McGraw-Hill, 1982. The book tells the story of a child named "X" whose sex is not revealed. The story humorously illustrates many gendered customs in our culture that children encounter. To the endless questions of "We still want to know what 'X' is!" the answer finally is, "You'll all know one of these days, and you won't need us to tell you!" Great reading for children three and older. Of particular interest to seven- to nine-year-olds!

84. Support girls' games by participating in them yourself and explaining their value to children.

Traditional girls' games are not highly valued forms of play in our culture, and boys and men rarely join in.

Sometimes it helps to emphasize the skills these games encourage. It is amazing how much more interested in sewing, craft work, and games like pick-up sticks boys become when it is pointed out that these activities develop finger muscles. This may seem to be bowing to sex role stereotypes about who should be building muscles, but everyone seems to benefit.

Some of the skills girls' games offer:

- Doll play: nurturing and empathy skills; manual dexterity and concentration (from the manipulation of tiny doll clothes)

- Jump rope: aerobic strength, rhythm, rhyming

- Jacks: manual dexterity, grouping of numbers with remainders

- Pick-up sticks: manual dexterity and concentration

- Hopscotch: balance

- Dress up: role playing, empathy

- Paper dolls: small muscle dexterity; scissor skills; concentration; empathy

Girls gain pride in skills like manual dexterity and the ability to concentrate, which really do help to put them ahead when they start school. Boys get a chance to participate in activities that they are often subtly guided away from.

85. When children notice sexism and it bothers them, encourage them *to write* to the editors of newspapers and magazines or to a manufacturer.

For example, the cover of an issue of *Time* has splashy artwork and the title "How Man Began" followed by an article about early hominids. As your daughter reads through it, she realizes that *all* the illustrations, and most of the pronouns, are male, even though "Lucy" *(Australopithecus afarensis)* is one of the most important research finds. The article is clearly meant to be about humans, since "mankind" is used interchangeably with "humanity."

A letter from a child may have more meaning for the recipient company than anything a parent could write, and it gives the child practice in letter writing and citizenship skills. The company should realize that at least two family members were involved (the child and one supervising adult). The letter might even be printed in the "Letters to the Editor" column of the publication.

86. Teach daughters how to take care of themselves so that they can have the freedom to go wherever boys would be allowed to go.

Specifically:

- Teach them to carry and how to use First Aid kits.

- Teach them to carry and how to use bike repair kits, and when they are old enough to drive, a road emergency kit and how to change a tire.

- Teach them to travel in groups. You may have to encourage similar attitudes on the part of other parents so that other girls in your daughter's circle of friends are similarly prepared.

- Teach them to plan their trips or outings and to designate call-in checkpoints.

- Encourage a level of alertness, a confident posture and demeanor, and an attitude of self-assurance that shows in their stride. Criminals *choose* victims and prefer to approach people who look as though they will be passive.

- Remember that boys are molested almost as often as girls. Teach sons to follow the same safety procedures.

A great book to start young kids (5–12) on the road to competence is *Playing It Smart: What to Do When You Are on Your Own: A Kid's Guide to Handling the In's and Out's of Everyday Life,* by Tova Navarra, New York: Barron's Educational Series, 1989, 124 pages.

87. Advise children on how to respond to sexual harassment.

Children need to know that, while they are not responsible for being harassed, under many sexual harassment policies they *are* responsible for telling the harasser that the behavior is unwelcome.

There are pamphlets, books, and often school policies that articulate what constitutes sexual harassment (anything that makes the recipient uncomfortable) and procedures that should be followed. Ideally, schools should *explain* their sexual harassment policies to students so there are no misunderstandings. Often students must make it clear, either verbally or in writing, that they did not welcome the behavior, that it offended them, and that they expect it to stop. The institution won't be able to help very much if the harasser doesn't realize that this behavior is causing a problem.

Parents of quiet children might have them rehearse what they would say, and how loudly they should respond, to unwelcome behavior. Just as parents have children rehearse what they should say if someone touched them in a way that makes them uncomfortable, actual practice might help a quiet child to come up with the words at the right moment. (See Tip #40.)

88. Explain to your young child or teenager that old-fashioned dating is, well, old-fashioned.

The idea that boys should do all the choosing and the asking and the paying is out-dated. Girls need some spending money, either earned or supplied, so that they experience a feeling of independence and are not in the position of feeling obligated to others.

Dates, which are really joint excursions, are better based, at least in part, on mutual interests. Encourage teenagers to join clubs and groups that share common interests as a way of meeting prospective dates.

Reprinted by permission of Bülbül—Gen Guracar.

seven

Public Proactive Steps

What you will find in this chapter:

- Tips for parents who want to do even more

- Lobbying for change

- Adult interactions

89. If you are trying to raise the consciousness of someone who has just stated that he or she has nothing in common with the opposite gender, try focusing on *interests* that they do share.

Comments by adults suggesting that they have nothing in common with the opposite gender are particularly influential to children who overhear them. We must try to raise the consciousness of adults when they make observations such as:

*"I don't want to go to the PTA meeting because it will be **all women** there."*

or:

*"I don't want to go to the athletic association meeting because it will be **all men** there."*

In such a case you might try asking sincerely, "Why do you think that you won't have anything in common with the people there?" pointing out common motivations in attending and participating in such an event.

90. Make it a personal policy not to tolerate sexist jokes or remarks within your earshot—especially in front of minors. It's as easy to remember as *the Golden Rule.*

You wouldn't tolerate conversational racism, would you?

If a man makes a crude sex-object remark about a woman, imagine that it's your daughter or sister that he's talking about. Now picture *your* daughter or sister with *his* son.

Would the man be likely to be speaking that way about his mother or sisters?

It's got to stop somewhere. If a remark would be inappropriate for a mother or sister, it is probably not respectful enough for any other woman or girl.

91. Give public credit—a word, a smile, a letter—to men who honor the tradition of fatherhood by nurturing children, both in their homes and in their communities. Your children will see you do it and learn from your example.

92. We must help both children and adults to see the unhealthy and *unrealistic* beauty images our society perpetuates for women and girls through commercial mass media.

Barbie's measurements in inches, if she were human, would be 40-18-32, and her permanently arched feet would be size 3, too small to support her tall body. Barbie is so popular that in most toy stores she has an entire aisle devoted to her, unlike any other toy or character. Girls, especially white girls, learn very early what the most desirable body form is in our culture.

Actors like Cher, Jane Fonda, and Raquel Welch, who are reported to have had cosmetic surgery, silicone implants, or ribs removed, or to use body doubles and then sell exercise videos, give children and adults the impression that this type of woman's body is attainable—if we would just have more *will power!* In another context, this might be spelled *f-r-a-u-d*.

Photographs and TV images are routinely computer-enhanced. This is why we don't see anyone who looks like Cindy Crawford in the grocery store. In reality, only one in ten thousand women has a body that would fit the image of a top fashion model, and even then, the images are cleaned-up to achieve perfection!

This is not true for male images. Movie heroes like Clint Eastwood, Kevin Costner, and even Michael Keaton don't have bodies or faces that would be unusual for many young men.

As a result of this double standard, even after they go to extra effort and expense, only 28 percent of women consider themselves attractive, compared to 42 percent of men. A majority of girls in elementary school like themselves, but by high school almost 75 percent no longer like themselves the way they are. Eating disorders and diets have become epidemic, and at earlier and earlier ages.

We need to help children identify false advertising and unrealistic promises in toy commercials. We also need to help children recognize

 the *unrealistic* beauty standards used to sell products in TV commercials and magazines. Advertisements suggest that women's normal bodies, eyes, lips, hair, and smell are not good enough as they are, so women need to buy diet food and drinks, makeup, hair bleach, color, and conditioners, and perfumes. We also need to encourage children and teens to question whether these products will actually make the user look like the advertised image.

Realistically–proportioned doll vs. fashion doll
Reprinted with the permission by Esteem International, Inc.

93. Lobby for legislation that will make gender bias in public schools a thing of the past (see page xviii). Remind legislators and school board officials that *over half* of the nation's students are affected. If legislation is passed, monitor its implementation.

Title IX of the Civil Rights Act, outlawing sex discrimination in public schools that receive federal funding, was passed in 1972. In 1974, the Women's Educational Equity Act was passed to help provide research, materials, and training to enable schools to comply with Title IX. An office was set up, grants were awarded, and research was begun.

After the 1980 election the Reagan administration moved swiftly to terminate all grants for the study of gender equity issues in the schools, stopping most research before it could be completed. The Women's Educational Equity office budget was slashed by 95 percent and its staff reassigned. As a result, not one school lost money from the Federal Government because of non-compliance with Title IX between 1972 and 1991. This is why there was so little progress during this period.

For a status report on any national education legislation regarding gender discrimination and bias subscribe to "Action Alert" from the American Association of University Women Program and Policy Department (202) 785-7712 or contact any of the other education organizations listed at the end of Chapter 3.

94. Does your school own a video camera on a tripod so that teachers can record themselves and monitor their interactions in class? If not, perhaps you can arrange for a community organization to lend or donate one.

Teachers need to have a chance to evaluate their own teaching, adjust their techniques, and monitor their personal progress. A video camera on a tripod allows teachers to tape themselves in their classroom and then review their performance in verbal and nonverbal interactions with students.

The final test is to have a colleague come in to observe, record, and score a teacher's classroom interactions. Ways of measuring this are available from educational research institutions or can be found in the *Sex Equity Handbook for Schools* by Myra and David Sadker, New York: Longman, 1982. Educational scorecards rate which children the teacher called on and what kind of feedback each child received. Teachers can clearly see whether they are proportioning time and encouragement equally.

(As an alternative, *audio* tapes can provide important feedback.)

95. Think globally, act locally! If your local newspaper doesn't give equal billing to girls' and boys' sporting events, write a letter to the editor suggesting that it should. Or, take your own pictures and submit them to the paper with captions. Local papers are generally very glad to print them.

Our most obvious games, the ones announced hourly on the radio, are professional sports. Women are achieving success in all the sports in which they are allowed to participate and are becoming more obvious in media coverage. But there is still a long way to go! When the sportscast comes on at the end of the news, the monologue rarely rattles off a string of girls' or women's game scores. And the culture still heavily favors sports in which men tend to excel. Such sports tend to emphasize body size as in football, or upper body strength as in baseball. A competitive event requiring strength and *agility* (like gymnastics or rock climbing), where women tend to excel, is not as popular.

Local newspapers are generally very responsive to community-interest stories. They will often print photos of girls' sports and of important events like Girl Scout projects; dance, gymnastics or ice skating competitions; and scholarship awards. What a great self-esteem builder for girls!

96. Ask that gender equity collections be established at your public and school libraries. If there is already a shelf of parenting books, ask that books on this subject be included.

While many books have been written in the last twenty years that have nonstereotypic characters, it is not always easy for parents or teachers to locate them quickly. Librarians and book reviewers have been compiling bibliographies of books that comply with multi-cultural concerns, a broader category, but have not dealt exclusively with gender stereotype issues for many years. With the renewed interest in gender bias, some libraries may agree to publish a bibliography list for the nonsexist texts in their system. Some will even mark the book bindings with stickers, a godsend for harried parents!

For those who have volunteer time or money to give, a donation to start the collection can help. Also, community groups such as the League of Women Voters and American Association of University Women can be approached for donations. A public ceremony in which the organization president donates a book or a check to the library is always welcome publicity for both the group and the library Gender Equity collection.

One library that has produced such a collection and is happy to share its database with other libraries is Mahopac Public Library, Mahopac, NY, (914) 628-2009. Requests must be in writing and on library letterhead.

97. If we really care about our children, we must lobby Congress to establish a *Children's* Public Broadcasting System.

Public television is great, but a few hours in the morning and in the afternoon is not enough for the differing ages and interests of America's children. We must offer children an alternative to the endless parade of violent children's cartoons and other shows designed only to sell accompanying products to children. Even as partisan support fluctuates for public television, both sides agree that public television for children is very important.

We can afford it. Our country spends more money on military bands than the *total* amount it spends on public television. Politicians are reluctant to propose an expansion of public television because they fear network reprisals at reelection time.

 Call the Capitol switchboard at (202) 224-3121 to reach your two Senators and your Representative in the House

 Boys Will Be Boys, Breaking the Link Between Masculinity and Violence, by Myriam Miedzian, Doubleday, 1991.

98. You *can* do something about sexist commercials: call the manufacturer's consumer line. If you see a sexist commercial for a product you like, say, your children's favorite cookies, go to the cupboard, pull out the box, and call the 800 consumer product telephone number. Explain that you like their product but will not want to buy it in future because . . . .

Marketing staffs *depend* on this feedback. Feedback from consumers is often printed and circulated around the company and ad agencies working on the product.

Call the 800 Directory: 1-800-555-1212. It will give you the 800 number for any company that has one.

The same can be done in response to magazines or mailed advertisements.

It only takes a minute, it's a lot better than being annoyed, and they *want* you to call, rather than lose your business. This is a great tip to teach teenagers!

99. Check whether United Way Fund allocations are distributed equally between programs for girls and programs for boys in your community.

In those that receive funding for girls, are the programs designed to really serve girls' needs? Organizations like Girls, Inc. and Girl Scouts, for example, are making a real effort to address gender-related issues.

How about youth employment programs? Are resources for employing both girls and boys allocated fairly?

100. At least several holidays and seasons of the year can draw attention to non-traditional gender contributions. Suggest these opportunities to a community organization to which you belong and schedule a program, perhaps also using the opportunity to honor a local individual.

Third Monday in January	**Martin Luther King, Jr.'s Birthday**
February 15th	**Susan B. Anthony's Birthday**
First Thursday in February	**National Girls and Women in Sports Day**
March (whole month)	**Women's History Month**
March 8th	**International Working Women's Day**
Fourth Thursday In April	**Take Our Daughters to Work Day**
August 26th	**Women's Equality Day:** the day women won the vote
October 24th	**United Nations Day**
Third Saturday in October	**BrotherPeace:** an International Day of Men Taking Action to End Men's Violence

Commemorative dates can be found in

 Chase's Calendar of Events, Chicago: Contemporary Books.

Some sources for planning a community event (see also the organizations listed below under Tip #101):

 Party goods, film rentals, and sources for *performers* can be obtained from National Women's History Project, Windsor, CA (707) 838-6000

 Posters on National Girls and Women in Sports Day can be obtained from Women's Sports Foundation, East Meadow, NY 1-800-227-3988

101. Join and/or financially support institutions that promote gender equality. Do it for your children and for your grandchildren!

Until women's accomplishments and contributions are more generously acknowledged and honored in all our cultural institutions, that is, in

- school curricula
- museum and library displays
- national holidays
- national currency
- patriotic traditions

there will continue to be a need for individual support of groups working to promote nonsexism. Until the contributions of men who nurture humanity in public and private ways are more prominently recognized and lauded, and until there is institutional recognition of the limitations imposed by traditional masculinity, we will need support groups that work toward these goals.

 National Women's Hall of Fame
Seneca Falls, NY (315) 568-8060

National Organization for Men Against Sexism (NOMAS)
San Francisco, CA (415) 546-6627

 The Ms. Foundation
New York, NY (212) 742-2300

 American Association of University Women
Washington, DC 1-800-326-AAUW

 National Organization for Women
Washington, DC (202) 331-0066

 Women's Sports Foundation
East Meadow, NY 1-800-227-3988

(See also the list of education organizations at the end of Chapter 3.)

Conclusion

It is hoped that this book has helped the reader to address gender bias in a variety of ways:

- in helping children to develop their full potential
- in monitoring micro-interactions with children
- in creating a network of supportive and empowering role models
- in teaching children a variety of skills, including coping skills.

Perhaps most important, it is hoped that this book has empowered parents and other caring adults to insist that elimination of gender bias become a priority issue in schools, children's most influential public experience.

Today's parents, who often both work outside the home, often rely on professional teachers and school administrators to provide the best and most current educational expertise that today's school budgets can afford. And this can be a fairly successful strategy, *except* when it comes to gender bias.

Schools can be very conservative places when educational issues and gender issues collide. Often, school administrators perceive their client to be the community at large that pays for school budgets, not the students. Even though there is overwhelming educational evidence that gender bias is a big problem, many schools wait for parents to ask before addressing gender bias.

Because gender concepts strike an emotional chord in many people, this issue is often perceived as one best left alone, unless parents raise the topic. Even though gender bias is not a monetary issue, even though gender bias affects the majority of students, even in states where the state education departments have mandated that gender bias be eliminated (see page xviii), this is one area where administrators frequently fail to initiate any action. Often, administrators still do not even consider gender as a category when they collect data about student performance.

It is important for adults to mention their concern to teachers, principals, coaches, school board members, and PTA members. It is important to seek out and support faculty who are implementing recommended changes inside classrooms and beyond in the greater school environment. It is important to ask questions at parent/teacher conferences and at school board elections. It is important that a *mission statement to eliminate gender bias is adopted.*

It's not as time consuming as it sounds. It's as easy as reading the math worksheets your children bring home from school and being alert when you chaperone a class trip or volunteer to help out in the classroom or with a PTA project. Parents have both the right and the responsibility, which schools encourage, to request education that helps each child to develop fully. May this book serve as a useful tool toward that end.

Appendix A: Nonbiased, Inclusive Language

In general

The use of *man* or *male* gender words to represent humanity collectively is ambiguous since it is not clear whether they refer to men only or also include women (and even children). Such usage implies that the entire species is male.

Example	Alternatives
man's achievement	human achievement
mankind	humanity, humankind, human civilization, all generations
man-made	synthetic, manufactured, artificial, imitation
manpower	human resources, work force, staffing, personnel
manned space flight	with crew, astronaut-controlled, piloted

unmanned space flight	mission/remote-controlled, crewless, unpiloted
man-hours	hours, hours worked, staff time, total hours, labor time
manhole	sewer/utility/access hole
man the phones	staff, operate
man-sized	big, sizable, extra large
brotherhood of man	bond of humanity, human kindness
common man, man in the street	ordinary person, common citizen
family of man	human race, civilization
goodwill to man	goodwill toward all, goodwill to humanity
layman	layperson, nonprofessional
modern man	modern civilization, modern peoples

Gender-specific words

Imply males even if females are also included.

Example	Alternatives
bachelor's degree	undergraduate degree
city fathers	city founders, city leaders/elders
forefathers	forebears, ancestors, predecessors
founding fathers*	the founders, patriots, colonial leaders
freshman	first-year student, frosh, first-semester student
gentlemen's agreement	informal, verbal, honorable
master's degree	graduate degree, advanced degree
mastermind	genius, brilliant creator

*If an all-male group, such as the writers of the Constitution, is meant, then the more specific description could be used. Similarly, if an all-female group is meant, the more specific description (foremothers) could be used.

Job titles

Most occupational and public office titles date from a time when only men performed these jobs. Contemporary women are involved in all occupations, making gender-labeled titles discriminatory. Occupational titles should now describe the job, not the person who does the job.

Example	Alternatives
airline steward, -ess	flight attendant
alderman	council member, ward representative, alder member
anchorman	anchor, news anchor
businessman	specify: executive, wholesaler, business person
cameraman	camera operator/technician, cinematographer, camera crew
chairman	chair, head, chairperson, convener
committeeman	committee member, representative
congressman	member of Congress, representative
councilman	councillor, council member, board member

craftsman	specify: carpenter, artisan, skilled craftworker
draftsman	draftsperson, designer, drafter
fireman	fire fighter
fisherman	angler, fisher
foreman	supervisor, superintendent
handyman	odd jobber, caretaker, odd-job worker
journeyman	journey worker, certified artisan, specify: iron worker
landlord	land owner, building owner, property manager
lineman	line worker, installer
mailman	mail carrier, letter carrier, postal worker
maintenance man	maintenance worker, custodian, janitor
paperboy	paper/newspaper carrier
policeman	officer, police officer, peace officer, law enforcement officer
salesman	salesperson, sales representative, salesclerk, clerk

spokesman	spokesperson, speaker
workmen	workers, laborers
weatherman	forecaster, meteorologist, weather reporter

Gender-specific job titles

Neither sex has a monopoly on jobs or the designations that go with them (except wet nurse and sperm donor!).

Example	**Alternatives**
female surgeon	surgeon
housewife	homemaker
lady doctor	doctor
male nurse	nurse
meter maid	parking enforcement/traffic officer
woman lawyer	lawyer

Words with *man* in the middle

Example	**Alternatives**
craftsmanship	artisanry, artistry, expertise
penmanship	script, handwriting, longhand

| sportsmanship | fairplay, sporting behavior, honorable competition, good sport |
| workmanship | skilled craft work, artisanship, artisanry, expertise |

Phrases that assume readers or listeners are male

Example	Alternatives
black tie gala	semiformal
convention goers and their wives	and their spouses/partners
you and your wife	you and your spouse/partner

Gender–specific words that perpetuate myths and attitudes

Example	Alternatives
lady luck	luck
maiden name	birth/given name, surname
maiden voyage	first, premier
master bedroom	main, largest, specify location: northeast

old wives' tale	legend, folklore, folk tale
tomboy	active/athletic/boisterous/adventurous/child
woman's intuition	intuition, hunch

Parallel titles

Treat men and women in a parallel manner when the description involves titles, jobs, and marital status.

Example	Alternatives
James Jones and Mrs. Jones	James and Mary Jones, Ms. and Mr. Jones
man and wife	husband and wife, man and woman

Feminine suffixes

Most English nouns can be used for either gender. Feminine suffixes such as *-ess, -trix, -ine* are unnecessary and seem to imply that the feminine variation is a lesser version of the masculine.

Example	Alternatives
actress	actor

authoress	author
executrix	executor, administrator
governess	tutor, instructor, teacher
heroine	hero
hostess	host
poetess	poet
priestess	priest
waitress	waiter, server

The suffix *-ette* is a diminutive signifying imitation (flannelette), small size (dinette) (operetta), or something of less importance, and thus should not be used to refer to females.

Example	**Alternatives**
bachelorette	woman
majorette	drum major, baton twirler
suffragette	suffragist
usherette	usher

Replacing male gender pronouns

The masculine pronoun *he* fails to represent the female *half* of the human species. Shown below are suggested solutions (as illustrated in the sentence, "Everyone is expected to do *his* job well").

- Pluralize:

  "The employees are expected to do *their* jobs well."

- Use indefinite pronouns:

  "Everyone is expected to do *a* good job."

- Use a double pronoun construction:

  "An employee is expected to do *her* or *his* job well."

- Use *they* as singular with indefinite pronouns (this is becoming more acceptable in speech, but is still considered substandard in writing):

  "Everyone is expected to do *their* job well."

- Replace gender-specific pronouns with *someone, anyone, one, the one, no one:*

  "One is expected to do one's job well."

Words that can be mistaken as sexist, but are not

These common words contain *man, male, his,* and *boy.* Because of their appearance, these words *look* as if they are male gender words, although they are actually derived from other, nongendered terms.

- ***human/humanity/humankind:*** from the Latin *homo* meaning human being

- **manual/manufacture/manager/mandate/manacle/maneuver:** from the Latin for *hand*

- **female:** from the Old French *femelle* from the Latin for *woman, femina*

- **history:** from the Greek word *historia,* from a root meaning to know, to inquire, to learn

- **boycott:** eponym derived from the name of Charles C. Boycott, an unpopular nineteenth–century English estate manager in Ireland

For further help with unconscious language bias, consult one of the reference books available in public, college, or school libraries, such as:

 The Dictionary of Bias-Free Usage: A Guide to Nondiscriminatory Language, by Rosalie Maggio, Phoenix: Oryx Press, 1991, 293 pages.

cathy®

by Cathy Guisewite

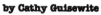

Appendix B:
Research Summaries

Nature versus nurture

Over the years, widely publicized studies have claimed scientific proof of behavioral, biologically–based differences between the genders.

- *Boys excel in mathematical ability.*

- *Girls have greater verbal ability than boys.*

- *Boys excel in visual-spatial ability.*

- *Males are more aggressive than females.*

- *Differences in the left and right hemispheres of the brain explain the differences in male and female behavior.*

- *The left (male) hemisphere controls analysis, computation, and verbal skills. The right (female) hemisphere controls visual skills, musical ability, and Gestalt processing.*

- *Natural Selection and Evolution prove the innate biological basis of our gender stereotypes.*

- *Female hormones cause women to be more emotional than men and to exhibit premenstrual syndrome (PMS).*

- *A hormone bath in utero is the point at which sex differences in behavior are determined.*

- *There are genes that cause sex differences in behavior.*

- *Testosterone in males causes aggression and the competitive nature that makes men better at sports, business, fighting, and dominating.*

Upon review by the scientific community, these conclusions and the experiments on which they are based have been seriously challenged. As a result, few major child development experts advise parents to look for inherent behavioral differences between the sexes.

While it is possible that there may be biological behavioral differences that are predictable between the two groups (although not predictable for individuals) such studies will continue to be hampered by common problems:

- There has never been a control group. The subjects studied have all been raised in cultures that socialize males and females to different standards.

- The researchers who define the studies, make the observations, and draw the conclusions have also been raised in biased cultures.

- For every trait studied so far, *the differences within each gender are greater* than the average differences between the genders.

- The *cause* of differences in behavior has not yet been identified, including whether *expectations* themselves are the cause.

Analysis of all the above well-publicized studies can be found in the highly recommended and readable book:

Myths of Gender: Biological Theories about Women and Men, by Dr. Anne Fausto-Sterling, New York: Basic Books, 2nd ed. 1992, 310 pages. (See also the reviews of this book in *Book Review Digest,* the resource librarians use in choosing reference books.)

Parents interested in the nature versus nurture question will find this book to be well worth the time and it may also help them to assess the significance of future studies.

And in visual form there is

A video set on the nature versus nurture topic, *The Opposite Sex,* by Film Australia, 1993, (4 hrs.) available from A&E Home Video
Ordering Department 1-800-423-1212

What the research shows

The following summary information has been heavily drawn from The Wellesley College Center for Research on Women's *The AAUW Report: How Schools Shortchange Girls;* Drs. Myra and David Sadker's *Failing at Fairness;* and Dr. Anne Fausto-Sterling's *Myths of Gender,* recommended above. Additional sources can be found following the appendixes.

Socialization at Home

What has been learned from analyzing the many scientific studies about the "nature" of behavior is that socialization has a greater influence on behavior than was previously suspected. Socialization studies show that adults tend to treat children of "opposite" genders differently, and to allow children to treat each other differently, according to stereotypic norms.

Following, in a condensed form, are the results of many different socialization studies about the nurture of children in the child's most important environment, the home. (It is important to note that the research focuses primarily on white, middle-class girls and boys. The effects of race, ethnicity, and socioeconomic class on gender development have not yet been adequately studied.)

- Before a child is even born, both mothers and fathers prefer to have a son for a firstborn or only child. Perhaps more telling than stated preferences (which are not very socially acceptable) is the fact that three out of four women stated that they *believed* that they were carrying boys. After birth, three times as many mothers of sons said they were "overjoyed" with the sex of their baby.

- One-day-old infants show exact, prolonged segments of movement correlating precisely in time with the speech patterns and rhythm of the adults talking to them.

- Mothers are more likely to repeat or imitate vocalizations from a girl baby than from a boy baby.

- Mothers are more likely to try to distract a male infant by dangling some object in front of him.

- Parents stimulate gross motor behavior in male infants more often than in females.

- Parents tend to hold daughters and sons differently, with boys pointed outward, girls facing inward, toward their parents' bodies.

- Adults select toys for (rubber hammer or doll) and play with an unfamiliar baby differently, according to which sex they are told it is. If they are *not* told the sex, they choose a neuter toy (a ball).

- When adults are asked to picture an intelligent child, 57 percent of women and 71 percent of men picture a boy.

- Parents are more concerned with appropriate sex typing (play attitudes and general behavior) in boys than in girls.

- Even sophisticated, professional parents praised two- and three-year-old daughters playing with dolls differently from the way they praised sons playing with dolls. Parents of daughters suggested that the children were rehearsing mothering roles. Parents of sons did not similarly encourage their two- and three-year-old sons to think of themselves as future fathers. Both were unaware of the difference in treatment.

- Fathers are more likely to have stereotypic expectations for their children than mothers.

- Parents, particularly fathers, mete out more physical punishment to boys than to girls.

- Both mothers and fathers express more warmth, use more emotional words, and are more likely to talk about sad feelings and events with girls.

- Parents (and teachers) underestimate the intelligence of girls. Girls can achieve, they believe, but they have to *try* harder.

- Fathers talk more with male children.

- Parents allow adolescent boys greater freedom than they allow adolescent girls.

- Mothers (but not fathers) allow teenage sons to challenge their authority, conceding in arguments to allow a son to practice using his own judgment. Neither concedes to teenage girls.

- When both parents work outside the home, teenage girls average ten hours per week on chores, teenage boys only three hours per week.

- Both parents interrupt daughters more than sons.

- A team of Canadian researchers concluded that parents continue to raise girls and boys in environments that are globally different. For example, parents give different toys to their children and do different kinds of activities with them; parents often decorate their rooms differently, dress them in different clothes, buy them different books, and rent different videos for them.

- Fathers who have become primary caregivers feel and express sex discrimination less acutely than do traditional fathers. Also, their sons show more curiosity and interest in the father as procreator or maker of human beings.

While many parents try not to be openly discriminatory, these studies show a pattern of *subtle* biases. Through many micro-interactions parents who consciously do not want their children trapped in stereotypes may unconsciously be conveying the opposite message. While individual parents may not fit these behavior patterns, this research is a valuable checklist.

Moreover, many parents, even well–educated ones, tell their children outright that girls and boys are different types of creatures, and that certain behaviors can be expected from one gender and not the other. Most children observe and contend with this too.

Children develop an interest in gender from age one-and-a-half to five and begin to experiment. Both male and female toddlers of mothers who never wear makeup or dresses will request nail polish, high heels, jewelry, lipstick, and hairdos. This is normal exploration. Boys, however, are stopped from stepping over gender boundary lines more often and more harshly, while girls are allowed wider freedom to be tomboys, a term almost unused today.

Boys are allowed much less freedom to be girl-like (all terms and concepts pertaining to girl-like are extremely negative). Not only is their maleness in question; since girls' behavioral characteristics are considered culturally inferior, they have doubly jeopardized their place by exhibiting such behavior and/or having such interests.

Many children are permitted and even encouraged to see each other as different, to feel that sharing interests and experiences with an opposite–sexed child is odd or even wrong, particularly after the preschool years. As children separate into gender-segregated groups, they begin to develop different language and play patterns.

Boys begin to play in larger groups, play structured games when together, and wisecrack and argue about the rules. Girls tend to play in groups no larger than four, are conciliatory about devising an activity that all want to participate in, and will dissolve a game in preference to having an argument about rules. It has been suggested that these gender-segregated play patterns evolve into differences in communication and interests that plague individuals later as adults, who must work and live together.

Research from School

Of late, much has been written about the unfairness of the school environment for girls, with some interest in negative effects on boys. Education, which constantly seeks improved results, produces a wealth of research. Current studies show that, while many gains were made over the last generation, there is still much that remains inequitable. Again, here are summaries of the research:

- Between the ages of three-and-a-half and five-and-a-half, boys stop responding to girls' requests, suggestions, and other attempts to influence them. When a girl and a boy compete for a toy, the boy dominates. Girls in a mixed (nursery school) classroom stay nearer to the teacher in order to have the teacher intercede. In single gender settings, girls play as independently as boys and sit farther from the teacher than boys in single gender settings do.

In studies of co-ed classrooms in grades K–12 these predominant patterns exist:

- Teachers call on boys more often than girls.

- Teachers allow boys to call out answers eight times more often than they allow girls to do so.

- Teachers give boys more time to answer questions (encouragement that they can get the answer).

- Teachers give boys more detailed feedback and criticism.

- Teachers encourage different attributes, such as thinking skills, in boys than in girls (for example, handwriting, obedience, and dependence on help).

- Male students are allowed to control the classroom conversation. They ask and answer more questions. They talk more and longer. They interrupt both female students and teachers.

- Male students are often allowed to take over limited space at school. They monopolize the classroom computer, the lunchroom tables, the playground space, and sometimes also the playground equipment.

In other studies:

- Girls' learning problems are not identified as often as those of boys, and girls are less likely to receive special education services. (Recent research reveals that dyslexia, the most common of the learning disabilities, is in fact as prevalent in girls as in boys.)

- Beyond elementary school the proportion of women teachers, especially in the sciences, tapers off. Thus, through middle school, high school, and college, girls have few mentors. (Mentors help students through the bumps and setbacks of their academic careers the way parents encourage adolescents. Male professors show an alarming tendency to sexually harass female students, especially at the college and graduate school level.

Even some of the most well meaning, dedicated, and effective teachers (like most adults) have difficulty purging the conditioning of society. In studies of classrooms, many excellent teachers who were trying to be very fair were aghast to watch videotapes of themselves, showing that, when their interactions with students were tallied, they had called on boys more often, given boys more and different kinds of encouragement, and reprimanded girls for the same behavior they overlooked in boys. Through a multitude of interactions throughout the hours and days and years in school, girls are receiving different lessons. The result is that, throughout their school years, girls receive less education—less in quality and less quantity of teacher time.

Even teachers who strive to allot their time fairly find that boys *demand* more attention. They arrive at school expecting to receive attention, and they get it. Many seemingly small inequities have a powerful cumulative impact. In the early grades girls are ahead of or equal to boys on almost every standardized measure of achievement and psychological well-being. By the time they graduate from high school or college, they have fallen back. Females are the only group in America to enter school ahead but leave behind. That this decline has received so little national attention is evidence of the pervasiveness of sexism in education.

Boys learn at school that they can demean girls at will. Many schools that do not permit racist, ethnic, or religious slights still tolerate sexism as harmless bigotry.

"Studies (show that adult) males who can call on a range of qualities, tenderness as well as toughness, are viewed by others as more intelligent, likable, and mentally healthy than rigidly stereotyped men. But boys cannot develop these repressed parts of themselves without abandoning attitudes that degrade girls," write researchers Myra and David Sadker of American University in their book *Failing at Fairness, How America's Schools Cheat Girls*. "Until gender equity becomes a value promoted in every aspect of school, boys, as victims of their own miseducation, will grow up to be troubled men; they will be saddened by unmet expectations, unable to communicate with women as equals, and unprepared for modern life" (1994, p. 225).

Girls have come a long way in school sports. In 1972, when Title IX was passed, 4 percent of girls participated in high school athletics. By 1987 their participation had grown to 26 percent. However, boys' participation in high school sports is still almost twice that of girls. Another consideration is that, since 1972, the percentage of women coaches has decreased, not increased, leaving girls with fewer female role models and mentors. In addition, male athletic coaches are more likely to develop sexual relationships with their female students.

In the American Association of University Women's study "Hostile Hallways" 76 percent of boys and 85 percent of girls report incidents of sexual harassment at school.

A disproportionate number of male high school and college athletes have been indicted in incidents of sexual assault and campus rape, suggesting that schools must take greater responsibility for the values students are learning.

School texts and curriculum content also contribute to the gender bias problem. When children use a history or science text that does not mention women, they learn that females are lesser beings. Some brand new history textbooks still devote only 2 to 3 percent of their space to women. Unless an individual teacher or school has made a concerted audit of all curricula for gender bias, females are usually *missing* from curriculum presented to girls and to boys. Science texts, math workbooks, standardized tests, and reading materials feature more boys and more examples of activities boys tend to be more familiar with; when both are pictured, they show boys doing *more* and girls doing *less*. Multiculturalism was supposed to include women. In many cases it has only postponed their inclusion while adding ethnic males.

Teachers, especially in the elementary grades, are still mostly women (72 percent). Administrators are still mostly men (principals 72.3 percent, superintendents 95.2 percent). Many have chosen their careers for traditional reasons and are seldom exposed to the outside world of American business. To date, many administrators have not even included gender as a category when they collect data about student performance.

Since 1983, when the U.S. Department of Education published *A Nation at Risk,* thirty-five prestigious Special Education Commissions have issued thirty-five special reports. The administrators serving on the commissions were overwhelmingly male. Aside from teenage pregnancy, the issue of gender was mentioned in only one report (a co-chair of that particular commission was female). That lone report suggested that commitment to Title IX be renewed. *America 2000,* issued by the Department of Education and President Bush in 1991, contained *no* gender specific recommendations.

Research on how children are faring

It is assumed that the younger generation embraces the values of equality in ways that children twenty years ago could barely imagine. But children are still raised in an environment loaded with subtle gender messages, and studies reveal what they think of themselves and of the opposite gender.

Studies by Myra and David Sadker of 1,100 schoolchildren in Michigan between 1988 and 1990 showed that, while 42 percent of girls could see some advantages to being a boy, 95 percent of boys could see *no* advantage to being a girl. Many expressed revulsion at the thought of themselves as a girl instead of a boy. These responses and results have recurred wherever the Sadkers pose the question. Clearly, girls and boys perceive themselves as very different.

Charol Shakeshaft of Hofstra University has been administering surveys to thousands of Long Island children of all ages, backgrounds, and socioeconomic groups for the past thirteen years. She asks them to complete the following sentence:

"If I woke up tomorrow and I was a girl (instead of a boy) or a boy (instead of a girl), I would . . . "

In thirteen years she has seen virtually *no change* in the answers.

They are:

"If I were a girl, then I would not be able to . . . "

"If I were a boy, I would be able to . . . "

The girls' answers typically reflect expanded opportunities for boys. The boys' answers reflect diminished opportunities for girls. This includes some girls saying things like "If I were a boy, then I would be able to be a medical doctor." Twenty percent of boys respond that they would commit suicide, but girls do not say this. These kinds of surveys yield the same kinds of results all around the country.

In a July 1994 *New York Times* survey, a majority of girls (57 percent) reported that most of the girls they know consider themselves to be equal to boys. Forty-two percent of girls responded that most of the girls they know think boys are better than girls. A majority of boys (59 percent) reported that most of the boys they know consider themselves to be better than girls. In the same survey, 86 percent of girls said that they expect to work outside the home while married and 7 percent said they did not. Among boys, 58 percent said that they expect their wives to work, and 19 percent expect a traditional, stay-at-home wife.

Research on girls

- Beginning in middle school, many girls deliberately curtail their classroom aggressiveness in deference to boys so that they will be better liked.

- Eating disorders (such as bulimia and anorexia nervosa) among girls in middle, high school, and college are rampant and increasing. It has been suggested that 80 percent of fourth–grade girls have already tried a diet.

- Adolescent girls suffer a self-esteem slide in middle and high school far greater than boys do. In elementary school 67 percent of boys and 60 percent of girls say they are happy the way they are. By high school, 46 percent of boys and 29 percent of girls say they are happy the way they are.

- SAT scores for girls do not predict how well girls do in high school or college, as measured by their grades. (SATs are often an important basis for scholarships and college admissions, however.)

- In Lewis Terman's studies of gifted men and women, boys' IQs fell 3 points during adolescence; girls' dropped a remarkable 13 points.

- Even top-ranked high school girls harbor deep-rooted doubts about their intellectual ability as they move through college. A study of male and female high school valedictorians who all felt that their intelligence was far above average showed that by senior year of college, 23 percent of the males still described themselves

Our scientific studies show that hormones affect the brain, so men are better at the higher–paying jobs and women are better with tedious, low-paying detail work.

Reprinted by permission of Bülbül—Gen Guracar.

this way. Even though their grades were slightly higher, none of the females still felt this way.

- One in ten teenage girls becomes pregnant each year. Unlike boys, when girls drop out of school, they usually stay out.

- When girls opt not to take higher math, science, and computer technology courses in high school, a chain reaction begins.

  - They have lower scores on standardized achievement tests.

  - They are then less likely to get scholarship money.

  - They are less likely to go to one of the more select coed colleges, as many of these colleges also limit the number of women they accept. Mentorship and networking from college is often an important contribution to future business success. Females are more likely to attend junior or community colleges.

  - They are also then limited in the subjects that they can later choose to study in college or graduate school (which is sometimes when a student realizes what field she or he wants to pursue).

  - Girls who wish to attend graduate and professional schools also score lower on the standardized graduate school admissions tests.

  - They are then prevented from entering higher-paying fields, which are also those requiring higher math.

- While girls are entering college in higher numbers than boys, they continue to pursue traditional fields such as liberal arts, education, health sciences, foreign languages, communications, psychology, and the performing arts. Almost 70 percent of the students who major in physics, chemistry, and computer science continue to be male. They similarly dominate the fields of engineering (85 percent), theology (75 percent), philosophy (64 percent), agriculture (69 percent), and architecture (61 percent).

Research on boys

The world for boys does not offer perfect prospects. Studies show that

- Some boys are the admired academic and sports heroes in high school, but in a hierarchical, pyramid model only a few can be at the top. Boys are also heavily represented at the very bottom of the pyramid. Boys in the middle and bottom constantly compete and many remain feeling unsuccessful and frustrated. In general, boys have lower report card grades.

- Boys are more likely to have trouble adjusting to school. By middle school, boys are more likely to be grade repeaters and drop-outs.

- Boys are more likely to be in special education programs. While some suggest that poor behavior lands some boys there (and quiet girls who also have problems are overlooked), current figures show that boys represent 58 percent in classes for the mentally retarded, 71 percent in classes for the learning disabled, and 80 percent in programs for the emotionally disturbed.

- Boys are the ones who stand out for discipline problems. When they have trouble with academics they often act out in destructive ways, gaining attention but for the wrong reasons. Boys, more than girls, are juvenile delinquents. They receive 71 percent of all school suspensions.

- Boys commit suicide two to three times more frequently than girls. Males use guns to commit suicide more frequently than females.

- Of children under eighteen arrested for violent crimes, 87 percent are boys.* Of those, 70 percent are fifteen to seventeen, and 30 percent are under fifteen. Of adult prison inmates (94 percent male), close to 40 percent were labeled as having learning disabilities and 30 percent are mildly retarded (there is some overlap between these two groups).

- Boys die more often because they have higher accident rates. Teenage boys are more likely to die from gunshot wounds than all natural causes combined. Eighty percent of all spinal cord injuries in the United States occur in males. In the fifteen- to twenty-four-year-old age group, boys die of accidents almost four times more often than girls.

* In one fifteen-year study of teenage and adult male criminal offenders, the most frequently given reasons for committing crimes were "I wanted them to know that I was no sissy" and "I had to prove that I was a man." The author of the above study, David Rothenberg, notes, however, that "child abuse, racism, drugs and alcohol habits, and poverty are at the top of lists about anti-sociability. Yet daughters grow up in the same homes as sons. But the young girls rob, steal, and kill with one tenth the frequency as their male counterparts."

- Boys have the highest insurance rates because they have the highest automobile accident and death rates. Twice as many boys aged sixteen to nineteen die in cars than girls, and young men aged twenty to twenty-nine die in cars at three times the rate of young women of the same age.

- Boys are three times more likely to become alcohol dependent and 50 percent more likely to use illicit drugs.

- Boys aged fifteen to nineteen are much more likely to be murdered than girls of the same age group. (White males are three times more likely to be murdered than white females. Black males are eight times more likely to be murdered than black females.)

Male violence in America is considered unfortunate but natural, genetic, the human norm, even though, in at least one cross-cultural study (Sanday 1981), 47 percent of the societies studied have no rape and in thirty-three of the cultures, both war and interpersonal violence are extremely rare.

Sources

Arnold, Karen D. 1992. "The Illinois Valedictorian Project: Academically Talented Women Ten Years after High School Graduation." Paper presented at the annual meeting of the American Education Research Association, San Francisco, April 24.

Askew, Sue, and Carol Ross. 1988. *Boys Don't Cry: Boys and Sexism in Education.* Philadelphia: Open University Press.

Bushwell, Kevin. 1994. "Turning Our Backs on Boys." *The American School Board Journal* (May): 20–25.

Condon, W. S., and L. W. Sander. 1974. "Neonate Movement Is Synchronized with Adult Speech: Interactional Participation and Language Acquisition." *Science* 183: 99–101.

Cramer, Robert E., et al. 1989. "Motivating and Reinforcing Functions of the Male Sex Role: Social Analogues of Partial Reinforcement, Delay of Reinforcement, and Intermittent Shock." *Sex Roles* 20: 551–73.

Dreifus, Claudia. "Sex with Professors." 1986. *Glamour,* August, 264–65, 308–9, 311.

Duke, D. L. 1976. "Who Misbehaves? A High School Studies Its Discipline Problems." *Educational Administration Quarterly* 12: 65–85.

Dweck, Carol, William Davidson, Sharon Nelson, and Bradley Enna. 1978. "Sex Differences in Learned Helplessness: II. The Contingencies of Evaluative Feedback in the Classroom; III. An Experimental Analysis." *Developmental Psychology* 14: 268–76.

Dziech, Billie Wright, and Linda Weiner. 1984. *The Lecherous Professor: Sexual Harassment on Campus.* Boston: Beacon Press.

Eagle, Carol J., and Carol Colman. 1993. *All That She Can Be: Helping Your Daughter Achieve Her Full Potential and Maintain Her Self-Esteem During the Critical Years of Adolescence.* New York: Simon and Schuster.

Earle, Janice. 1990. *Counselor/Advocates: Keeping Pregnant and Parenting Teens in School.* Alexandria, VA: National Association of State Boards of Education.

Fausto-Sterling, Anne. 1992. *Myths of Gender: Biological Theories About*

Women and Men. New York: Basic Books.

F.B.I. Uniform Crime Reports 1992 Arrest Figures. 1994. *The New York Times,* May 16, A1.

Glaser, Robert D., and Joseph S. Thorpe. 1986. "Unethical Intimacy: A Survey of Sexual Contact and Advances Between Psychology Educators and Female Graduate Students." *American Psychologist* 40: pp. 43–51.

Government Employees Insurance Company Communications Department. "Motor Vehicle Deaths per 100,000 people, 1993." *Surviving Driving: Five Steps to Safer Travel.* Source: National Highway Traffic Safety Administration.

Hendrick, Joanne, and Terry Stange. 1991. "Do Actions Speak Louder Than Words? An Effect of the Functional Use of Language on Dominant Sex Role Behavior in Boys and Girls." *Early Childhood Research Quarterly* 6: 565–76.

Holt, Robert R. 1987. *Converting the War System to a Peace System.* Unpublished paper prepared for a conference of the Exploratory Project on the Conditions of Peace, Cohasset, MA. (Includes cross-cultural study of war and interpersonal violence.)

Jackson, Donna. 1992. *How to Make the World a Better Place for Women—in Five Minutes a Day.* New York: Hyperion.

Kessler, R., and J. McRae. 1981. "Trends in the Relationship Between Sex and Psychological Distress, 1957–76." *American Sociological Review* 46.

Kimball, Meredith. 1989. "A New Perspective on Women's Math Achievement." *Psychological Bulletin* 105: 198–214.

Kimbrell, Andrew. 1991. "A Time for Men to Pull Together," *Utne Reader,* May–

June, 66–75.

Klein, Susan, and Karen Bogart. 1987. "Achieving Sex Equity in Education: A Comparison of Pre- and Post-Secondary Levels." *Equity and Excellence* 23: 114–22.

Kline, Bruce, and Elizabeth Short. 1991. "Changes in Emotional Resilience: Gifted Adolescent Females." *Roeper Review* 13: 118–21.

Kuebli, Janet, and Robyn Fivush. 1992. "Gender Differences in Parent-Child Conversations About Past Emotions." *Sex Roles* 27: 683–98.

Lerch, Steve. 1984. "The Adjustment of Athletes to Career Ending Injuries." *Arena Review,* March 4, 62.

Lester, David. 1992. *Why People Kill Themselves: A 1990's Summary of Research Findings on Suicide Behavior,* 3rd ed. Springfield, IL: Charles C. Thomas.

Maccoby, Eleanor E. 1990. "Gender and Relationships: A Developmental Account." *American Psychologist* 45: 516. (Refers to the work of Maltz and Borker [1982] and others.)

Maltz, Daniel N., and Ruth A. Borker. 1982. "A Cultural Approach to Male-Female Miscommunication." In *Language and Social Identity,* ed. John J. Gumperz, 196–216. Cambridge: Cambridge University Press.

Mann, Judy. 1994. *The Difference: Growing up Female in America.* New York: Warner Books, 23.

Martin, Carol Lynn. 1990. "Attitudes and Expectations About Children with Nontraditional Gender Roles." *Sex Roles,* 22: 151–65.

Miedzian, Myriam. 1991. *Boys Will Be Boys: Breaking the Link Between Masculinity and Violence.* New York: Doubleday.

Moss, H. A. 1974. "Early Sex Differences and Mother-Infant Interaction." In *Sex Differences in Behavior,* ed. R. C. Friedman, R. H. Richart, and R. L. Van de Wiele, 149–63. New York: Wiley.

Nagel, K. L., and Karen H. Jones. 1992. "Sociological Figures in the Development of Eating Disorders." *Adolescence* 27: 107–13.

Nelson, Janet. 1987. Report on National Safety Council Statistics on Accidental Deaths. *The New York Times,* March 1.

Office for Civil Rights. 1988. *1986 Elementary and Secondary Civil Rights Survey, State and National Summary of Projected Data.* Washington, DC: US Department of Education.

Office for Sex Equity in Education, Michigan Department of Education. 1990. *The Influence of Gender-Role Socialization on Student Perceptions: A Report Based on Data Collected from Michigan Public School Students* (rev. June).

Osborne, R. W. 1991. "Men and Intimacy: An Empirical Review." Paper presented at the American Psychological Association, San Francisco.

Persell, Caroline Hodges, Sophia Catsambis, and Peter W. Cookson, Jr. 1992. "Differential Asset Conversion: Class and Gendered Pathways to Selective Colleges." *Sociology of Education* 65: 208–25.

Pomerleau, Andree, Daniel Bolduc, Gerard Malcuit, and Louise Cossette. 1990. "Pink or Blue: Environmental Gender Stereotypes in the First Two Years of Life." *Sex Roles* 22: 359–68.

Pruett, Kyle D. 1987. *The Nurturing Father.* New York: Warner Books.

Ransom, Michael R. 1990. "Gender Segregation by Field in Higher Education." *Research in Higher Education* 31: 477–94.

Raty, Hannu, and Leila Snellman. 1992. "Does Gender Make Any Difference? Common-Sense Conceptions of Intelligence." *Social Behavior and Personality* 20: 23–34.

Rothenberg, David. 1993. "Out on a Limb." *Fortune News,* Spring.

Sadker, Myra, and David Sadker. 1994. *Failing at Fairness, How America's Schools Cheat Girls.* New York: Charles Scribner's Sons.

Sadker, Myra, and David Sadker. 1994. "Why Schools Must Tell Girls: You're Smart, You Can Do It." *USA Weekend,* February 4–6.

Sanday, Peggy. 1981. *Female Power and Male Dominance: On the Origins of Sexual Inequality.* Cambridge: Cambridge University Press. (Includes cross-cultural study of rape.)

Shakeshaft, Charol. 1993. "Gender and Schooling: What Parents and Teachers Should Know." Reported in a speech October 13. Scarsdale, NY.

Shaywitz, Sally, Bennett Shaywitz, Jack Fletcher, and Michael Escobar. 1990. "Prevalence of Reading Disability in Boys and Girls." *Journal of the American Medical Association* 264: 998–1002.

Sheldon, Amy. 1990. "Pickle Fights: Gendered Talk in Preschool Disputes." *Discourse Processes* 13.

Shepardson, Daniel, and Edward Pizzini. 1992. "Gender Bias in Female Elementary Teachers' Perceptions of the Scientific Ability of Students." *Science Education* 76: 147–53.

Siegal, Michael. 1987. "Are Sons and Daughters Treated More Differently by Fathers Than by Mothers?" *Developmental Review* 7: 183–209.

Smith, C., and B. B. Lloyd. 1978. "Maternal Behavior and Perceived Sex of

Infant." *Child Development* 49: 211–14.

Snyder, Thomas, and Charlene Hoffman. 1992. *Digest of Education Statistics 1992*. Washington DC: U.S. Dept. of Education 31: 477–94.

Spender, Dale. 1980. *Learning to Lose: Sexism and Education*. London: Women's Press.

Statistical Abstract of the United States, 1993. Washington, DC: U.S. Dept. of Commerce, Table 138.

Tavris, Carol. 1992. *The Mismeasure of Woman*. New York: Simon and Schuster.

Touchton, Judith G., and Lynne Davis with the assistance of Vivian Parker Makosky. 1991. *Fact Book on Women in Higher Education*. New York: Macmillan.

Vogel, Susan. 1990. "Gender Differences in Intelligence, Language, Visual-Motor Abilities, and Academic Achievement in Students with Learning Disabilities: A Review of the Literature." *Journal of Learning Disabilities* 23: 44–52.

Watts, W. David, and Loyd S. Wright. 1990. "The Relationship of Alcohol, Tobacco, Marijuana and Other Illegal Use to Delinquency Among Mexican-American, Black and White Adolescent Males." *Adolescence* 25: 171–81.

Weiss, Joan Solomon. 1985. *Raising a Son: The Essential Guide to a Healthy Mother-Son Relationship*. New York: Summit Books.

Wellesley College Center for Research on Women. 1992. *How Schools Shortchange Girls: The AAUW Report*. Washington, DC: American Association of University Women Educational Foundation.

Appendix C:
Famous Women in History

The following list is provided as *a starting point* for parents who need finger-tip information about famous women in history. Women already mentioned in the text are generally left off this list. Many, many more famous women will be found in reference volumes listed at the end of this section and in the Bibliography.

Jane Addams 1860–1935 founder of professional social work as we know it. Nobel Peace Prize recipient

Marian Anderson 1902–1993 African American operatic contralto, UN delegate

Mary Anderson 1859–1940 organizer Women's Trade Union League (textiles), Women's Bureau

Susan B. Anthony 1820–1906 founder National Woman Suffrage Association; organizer New York State Temperance Society, American Anti-Slavery Society, Women's Loyal National League: organized support for the Nineteenth Amendment

Hannah Arendt 1906–1975 German American philosopher and political theorist

Mary Ritter Beard 1876–1958 historian, co-author *The Rise of Ameri-*

can Civilization, suffragist

Ruth Benedict 1887–1947 anthropologist, author *Patterns of Culture* and *The Chrysanthemum and the Sword*

Mary McLeod Bethune 1875–1955 African American educator and civic leader; founder National Council of Negro Women, Daytona Normal and Industrial Institute for Negro Girls (Bethune-Cookman College); president American Teachers Association, Administrative Assistant for Negro Affairs in the Roosevelt Administration

Alice Stone Blackwell 1857–1950 feminist, organizer in temperance and trade unions, cofounder League of Women Voters of Massachusetts

Elizabeth Blackwell 1821–1910 first American woman doctor

Amelia Bloomer 1818–1894 feminist, suffragist, publisher of *The Lily,* published patterns for less restrictive women's clothing (derisively called bloomers)

Gertrude Bonnin 1875–1936 Native American author, reformer, teacher

Margaret Bourke–White 1905–1971 American photojournalist

Pearl Buck 1892–1973 humanitarian, author *The Good Earth*

Frances Cabrini 1850–1917 Italian American famous for establishment of social welfare institutions in Chicago

Maria Cadilla de Martinez 1886–1951 folklorist, writer, feminist

"Calamity" Jane (Martha Jane Canary) 1852–1903 famous and fabled woman of the American West

Rachel Carson 1907–1964 biologist, conservationist, author *Silent Spring,* catalyst of what has become the modern environmental movement

Mary Cassatt 1844–1926 American impressionist painter

Catherine II (Catherine the Great) 1729–1796 Russian Empress

Carrie Chapman Catt 1859–1947 national and international suffragist, founder Woman Suffrage Party and cofounder League of Women Voters

Marie Curie 1867–1934 Polish-French chemist, discoverer of radium and radioactivity, physicist

Julia de Burgos c.1914–1953 Puerto Rican-American poet of social injustice, nationalism, oppression of women, antiwar issues, journalist

Dorothea Dix 1802–1887 champion of the mentally ill, founder of the mental health field and the first state mental hospital in New Jersey, Civil War nurse

Abigail Duniway 1834–1915 Oregon pioneer and suffragist who founded a weekly women's rights newspaper

Amelia Earhart 1898–1937 airplane pilot, founder international organization of women pilots, the "Ninety-Nines"

Gertrude Ederle c.1906 German American, the first woman to swim the English Channel in 1926

Eleanor of Acquitane 1122–1204 English–French queen (married Henry II, Louis VII) hospital builder

Edna Ferber 1887–1968 playwright and novelist

Irmgard Flugge-Lotz 1903–1974 engineer and mathematician influencing the field of fluid mechanics

Elizabeth Gurley Flynn c.1830–1964 organizer for Industrial Workers of the World

Emma Goldman 1869–1940 advocate of birth control, free speech, anarchy

Mother Goose c.1648–1752? Elizabeth Foster Vergoose, American nursery-rhyme maker

Ella Grasso 1919–1981 Italian American governor of the state of Connecticut

Angelina Grimké 1805–1879 **and Sarah Grimké** 1792–1873 abolitionists and lecturers for women's rights

Charlotte Forten Grimké 1838–1904 African American author, educator, abolitionist, and social reformer

Jennie Grossinger 1892–1972 Austrian American hotel executive and philanthropist

Edith Hamilton 1867–1963 German-American classicist, author, and educator

Lorraine Hansberry 1930–1965 African American playwright, author *A Raisin in the Sun,* the first play by a black woman to appear on Broadway

Sonja Henie 1912–1969 Olympic medalist figure-skater, actor

Karen Horney 1885–1952 German American psychiatrist and psychoanalyst who stressed the importance of sociocultural factors in neuroses

Julia Ward Howe 1819–1910 poet "Battle Hymn of the Republic," lecturer, social reformer, abolitionist, founder Mother's Peace Day 1872

Anne Hutchinson 1591–1643 champion of religious freedom

Mahalia Jackson 1911–1972 African American gospel singer

Pattie Ruffner Jacobs 1875–1935 Alabama suffragist

Mary Harris (Mother) Jones 1830–1930 Irish American, Knights of Labor (mine workers) organizer

Helen Keller 1880–1968 blind and deaf author and feminist, advocate for the handicapped

Susan LaFleche-Picotte 1865–1915 Native American physician, hospital founder, and political organizer

Emma Lazarus 1849–1887 Jewish-American poet who wrote the inscription for the base of the Statue of Liberty, "Give me your tired . . ."

Lydia Kamekha Liliuokalani 1838–1917 last sovereign ruler of the Hawaiian Islands

Margaret Mead 1901–1978 American anthropologist and author

Golda Meir 1898–1978 American-born prime minister of Israel

Grandma (Anna Mary Robertson) Moses 1860–1961 American folk painter

Louise Nevelson c.1900–1988 Russian American sculptor

Florence Nightingale 1820–1910 English-American founder of the modern nursing profession in 1850s

Annie Oakley 1860–1926 champion sharpshooter and horseback rider

Rosa Parks 1913– African American civil rights champion

Alice Paul 1885–1977 English American lawyer, suffragist, social reformer, and feminist, author the Equal Rights Amendment in 1923

Molly Pitcher c.1754–1832 American Revolutionary War hero

Pocahontas 1595–1617 Native American princess and diplomat who interceded and served as an interpreter between the English and Native Americans in North America and England

Marjorie Merriweather Post 1887–1973 accomplished business person and philanthropist

Eleanor Roosevelt 1884–1962 prominent First Lady, UN delegate, leader in minority rights and the development of the *Declaration of Human Rights*

Sacagewea 1786–c.1812 Shoshone interpreter and guide who led Lewis and Clark to the Pacific Coast

Margaret Sanger 1883–1966 champion of birth control in America

Rose Schneiderman c.1884–1972 labor organizer and social reformer

Eleanora Sears 1881–1968 American horse rider, tennis player, feminist

Anna Howard Shaw 1847–1919 English American physician, minister, and suffragist organizer of Woman Suffrage Organization in Massachusetts

Mary Shelley 1797–1851 English poet and author of *Frankenstein* in 1816

Elizabeth Cady Stanton 1815–1902 giant of the women's rights and suffrage movements who called the famous Women's Rights Convention at Seneca Falls, NY, in 1848 and drafted its *Declaration of Sentiments*

Lucy Stone 1818–1893 abolitionist and suffragist who lectured for the American Anti-Slavery Society and called the first national women's rights convention in 1850

Maria Tallchief 1925– Native American ballet dancer

Mary Church Terrell 1863–1954 African American leader and educator, president National Association of Colored Women

Margaret Thatcher 1925– Prime Minister of England

Sojourner Truth 1797–1883 African American abolitionist, feminist, and reformer

Harriet Tubman c.1826–1913 African American champion of escaping slaves, Civil War scout

Loreta Janeta Velasquez c.1842–1897 Confederate soldier, male impersonator, Civil War spy

Phillis Wheatley 1753–1784 first African American female poet to be published in (colonial) America

Sarah Winnemucca 1844–1891 Native American political leader, author *Life among the Piutes: Their Wrongs and Claims,* army scout

Anna May Wong 1907–1961 Chinese–American actress

Victoria Clafin Woodhull 1838–1927 suffragist who asked Congress to legalize woman suffrage under the Fourteenth amendment, Presidential candidate, stockbroker

"Babe" Didrickson Zaharias 1914–1956 champion athlete track, field, and golf, founder Ladies Professional Golf Association

A complete reference book is:

Index to Women of the World, from Ancient to Modern Times, by Norma Olin Ireland, Scarecrow Press, 1988

This is handy to have because many, many famous women are not listed in the dictionaries or encyclopedias that families are likely to keep at home. Although not a large book, with an average of twenty entries per page it contains approximately fifteen thousand well-known women

Bibliography of Nonsexist Children's and Adult Reference Books

This list should be considered just a starting point for parents who are seeking resources.

Picture books

Babbitt, Natalie. 1968. *Phoebe's Revolt.* San Francisco: Collins Publishers.

Bach, Alice. 1978. *Millicent the Magnificent.* New York: Harper Row.

Baynton, Martin. 1988. *Jane and the Dragon.* London: Walker Books.

Bemelmans, Ludwig. 1939. *Madeline.* New York: Viking Press.

Bemelmans, Ludwig. 1977. *Madeline and the Gypsies.* New York: Puffin Books.

Brown, Drollene P. 1995. *Sybil Rides for Independence.* Morton Grove: Whitman.

Brown, Marc. 1981. *The True Francine.* Boston: Little Brown and Co.

Brown, Marc, and Laurene Krasney. 1984. *The Bionic Bunny Show.* New York: Little Brown and Co.

Burton, Virginia Lee. 1943. *Katy and the Big Snow.* Boston: Houghton Mifflin Co.

Caines, Jeanette. 1982. *Just Us Women.* New York: HarperCollins Childrens Books.

Coerr, Eleanor. 1988. *Chang's Paper Pony.* New York: HarperCollins Childrens Books.

Day, Marie. 1991. *Dragon in the Rocks.* Buffalo: Greey de Pencier Books.

De Paola, Tomie. 1979. *Oliver Button Is a Sissy.* San Diego: Harcourt/Brace.

De Paola, Tomie. 1974. *Watch Out for the Chicken Feet in Your Soup.* Englewood Cliffs: Prentice/Hall.

Fischer, Barbra, and Eberhard. 1986. *Gita Will Be a Dancer: A Picture Book for Children on Classical Indian Dance in English and Hindi.* New York: United Nations Children's Fund (UNICEF).

Gauch, Patricia Lee. 1971. *Christina Katerina and the Box.* New York: Coward, McCann and Geoghegan.

George, Jean Craighead. 1974. *All Upon a Sidewalk.* New York: E.P. Dutton.

Hall, Adelaide. 1969. *One Kitten for Kim.* Reading: Addison-Wesley.

Heyward, DuBose. 1939. *The Country Bunny and the Little Gold Shoes.* Boston: Houghton Mifflin.

Hoffman, Mary. 1991. *Amazing Grace.* Pittsburgh: Dial.

Isadora, Rachel. 1976. *Max.* New York: Macmillan.

Leaf, Munro. 1936. *The Story of Ferdinand.* New York: Viking Press.

Lillie, Patricia. 1989. *Jake and Rosie.* New York: Greenwillow Books.

Luenn, Nancy. 1990. *Nessa's Fish.* New York: Atheneum.

Martin, Charles E. 1986. *For Rent.* New York: Greenwillow Books.

McCully, Emily Arnold. 1992. *Mirette on the High Wire.* New York: Putnam Publishing Group.

Munsch, Robert N. 1980. *The Paper Bag Princess.* Buffalo: Annick Press.

Munsch, Robert N. 1991. *Millicent and the Wind.* Buffalo: Annick Press.

O'Brien, Anne Sibley. 1986. *It's Hard to Wait.* New York: Henry Holt and Co.

Piper, Watty. 1990. *The Little Engine That Could.* New York: Platt Munk.

Pomerantz, Charlotte. 1992. *The Princess and the Admiral.* New York: Feminist Press.

Quinlan, Patricia. 1987. *My Daddy Takes Care of Me.* Buffalo: Annick Press.

Schecter, Ellen. 1992. *The Warrior Maiden: A Hopi Legend.* New York: Bantam Books.

Stops, Sue. 1992. *Dulcie Dando, Soccer Star.* New York: Henry Holt.

Thompson, Kay. 1955. *Eloise.* New York: Simon and Schuster.

Waber, Bernard. 1972. *Ira Sleeps Over.* Boston: Houghton Mifflin.

Waddell, Martin. 1986. *The Tough Princess.* New York: Philomel Books.

Waxman, Stephanie. 1989. *What Is a Girl? What Is a Boy?* New York: T Y Crowell Junior Books.

Wells, Rosemary. 1973. *Noisy Nora.* New York: Scholastic Inc.

Yolen, Jane. 1995. *The Ballad of the Pirate Queens.* New York: Harcourt Brace.

Zolotow, Charlotte. 1972. *William's Doll.* New York: Harper and Row.

Easy/early readers

Bulla, Clyde Robert. 1987. *The Chalk Box Kid.* New York: Random House.

Coerr, Eleanor. 1981. *The Big Balloon Race.* New York: HarperCollins Childrens Books.

Hazen, Barbara Shook. 1992. *Mommy's Office.* New York: Atheneum Childrens Books.

Howe, James. 1990. *Pinky and Rex.* New York: Atheneum Childrens Books.

Howe, James. 1991. *Pinky and Rex and the Mean Old Witch.* New York: Atheneum Childrens Books.

Lobel, Arnold. 1979. *Days with Frog and Toad.* New York: HarperCollins Childrens Books.

Lobel, Arnold. 1972. *Frog and Toad are Friends.* New York: HarperCollins Childrens Books.

Penner, Lucille Recht. 1994. *The True Story of Pocahontas.* New York: Random House.

Juvenile biography

Aliki. 1989. *The King's Day: Louis XIV of France.* New York: T Y Crowell Junior Books.

Billings, Charlene W. 1989. *Grace Hopper: Navy Admiral and Computer Pioneer.* Hillside: Enslow Publishers.

Blair, Ruth Van Ness. 1975. *Mary's Monster (Mary Annings Discovery of Ichthyosaurus).* New York: Coward McCann and Geoghegan.

Brill, Ethel. 1946. *Madeline Takes Command.* New York: McGraw Hill.

Bryant, Jennifer. 1992. *Marjory Stoneman Douglas: Voice of the Everglades.* New York: Twenty–first Century Books.

Clayton, Ed. 1986. *Martin Luther King, The Peaceful Warrior.* New York: Pocket Books.

Cohen, Neil. 1992. *Jackie Joyner-Kersee.* Boston: Little, Brown and Co.

Faber, Doris. 1970. *A Colony Leader: Anne Hutchinson.* Champaign, Illinois: Garrad.

Federson, Lewis H. 1969. *Thurgood Marshall, Fighter for Justice.* New

York: McGraw Hill.

Giblin, James Cross. 1993. *Edith Wilson, The Woman Who Ran the United States.* New York: Viking Press.

Grant, Anne. 1976. *Danbury's Burning.* New York: David McKay Co.

Haviland, Virginia. 1952. *William Penn, Founder and Friend.* Nashville: Abington Press.

Kudlinski, Kathleen V. 1988. *Rachel Carson: Pioneer of Ecology.* New York: Puffin Books.

Leavell, J.P. Perry Jr. 1987. *Woodrow Wilson.* New York: Chelsea House.

Lewis, Claude. 1972. *Benjamin Banneker, The Man Who Saved Washington.* New York: McGraw Hill-Rutledge.

McPherson, Stephanie Sammartino. 1992. *I Speak for the Women: A Story of Lucy Stone.* Minneapolis: Carolrhoda Books, Inc.

McPherson, Stephanie Sammartino. 1990. *Rooftop Astronomer: A Story About Maria Mitchell.* Minneapolis: Carolrhoda Books, Inc.

Montegomery, Elizabeth. 1970. *Gandhi, Peaceful Fighter.* Champaign, Illinois: Garrard Publishing.

Moss, Nataniel. 1994. *Ron Kovic, Antiwar Activist.* Minneapolis: Chelsea House.

Nicholson, Michael. 1989. *Raoul Wallenberg: The Swedish Diplomat Who Saved 100,000 Jews Before Mysteriously Disappearing.* Milwaukee: Gareth Stevens Inc.

O'Connor, Barbara. 1993. *Mammolina: A Story About Maria Montessori.* Minneapolis: Carolrhoda Books.

Rappaport, Doreen. 1991. *Living Dangerously: American Women Who Risked Their Lives for Adventure.* New York: HarperCollins Childrens Books.

Richards, Dorothy Fay. 1978. *Abe Lincoln: Make It Right!* Elgin, Illinois: Children's Press.

Roop, Peter. 1985. *Keep the Lights Burning, Abbie.* Minneapolis: Carolrhoda Books.

Russell, Sharman Apt. 1988. *Frederick Douglass, Abolitionist Editor.* New York: Chelsea House.

Stevens, Bryna. 1984. *Deborah Sampson Goes to War.* Minneapolis: Carolrhoda Books.

Vare, Ethlie Ann. 1992. *Adventurous Spirit: A Story about Ellen Swallow Richards.* Minneapolis: Carolrhoda Books.

Wadsworth, Ginger. 1994. *Susan Butcher: Sled Dog Racer.* Minneapolis: Lerner.

Warner, Lucille Schulberg. 1976. *From Slave to Abolitionist: The Life of William Wells Brown.* New York: Dial Press.

Westman, Paul. 1983. *Andrew Young, Champion of the Poor.* Minneapolis: Dillion Press.

Juvenile fiction

Bagnold, Enid. 1949. *National Velvet.* New York: Morrow Junior Books.

Burroughs, Polly. 1968. *The Honey Boat.* New York: Little, Brown and Co.

Clapp, Patricia. 1977. *I'm Deborah Sampson—A Soldier in the War of the Revolution.* New York: Lothrop, Lee and Shepard.

Landon, Lucinda. 1987. *Meg MacKintosh and the Case of the Curious Whale Watch.* New York: Joy Street Books.

Landon, Lucinda. 1989. *Meg MacKintosh and the Mystery at the Medieval Castle.* New York: Joy Street Books.

Lindgren, Astrid. 1985. *Pippi Longstocking.* New York: Viking Press.

O'Dell, Scott. 1980. *Sarah Bishop.* Boston: Houghton Mifflin.

O'Dell, Scott. 1986. *Streams to the River, River to the Sea: A Novel of Sacagawea.* Boston: Houghton Mifflin Co.

Adult nonfiction

Anderson, Bonnie, and Judith Zinsser. 1988. *A History of Their Own: Women in Europe from Pre-history to Present Vol. 1 and 2.* New York: HarperCollins Publishers.

Askew, Sue, and Carol Ross. 1988. *Boys Don't Cry: Boys and Sexism in Education.* Philadelphia: Open University Press.

Barchers, Suzanne I., ed. 1990. *Wise Women: Folk and Fairytales from Around the World.* Englewood, Colorado: Libraries Unlimited, Inc.

Bingham, Mindy, and Sandy Stryker with Susan Allstetter Neufeldt. 1995. *Things Will Be Different for My Daughter.* New York: Penguin.

Forbes, Malcolm. 1990. *Women Who Made a Difference: 100 Fascinating Tales of Unsung Heroines and Little Known Stories of Famous Women Who Changed Their World and Ours.* New York: Simon and Schuster.

Gregorich, Barbara. 1993. *Women at Play: The Story of Women in Baseball.* San Diego: Harcourt, Brace and Co.

Heller, Nancy G. 1987. *Women Artists, An Illustrated History.* New York: Abbeville Pr. Inc.

James, Edward T., ed. 1971. *Notable American Women 1607–1950.* Cambridge: The Belknap Press of Harvard University Press.

Lester, Joan Steinau. 1994. *The Future of White Men and Other Diversity Dilemmas.* Emeryville: Conari Press.

Lunardini, Christine. 1994. *What Every American Should Know About Women's History: 200 Events That Shaped Our Destiny.* Bob Adams, Inc.

Macdonald, Anne L. 1992. *Feminine Ingenuity: Women and Invention in America.* New York: Ballantine Books.

McHenry, Robert, ed. 1980. *Famous American Women: A Biographical Dictionary from Colonial Times to the Present.* New York: Dover.

Pearson, Carol. 1981. *The Female Hero in American and British Literature.* New York: Bowker.

Salmonson, Jessica Amand. 1991. *The Encyclopedia of Amazons: Women Warriors from Antiquity to the Modern Era.* New York: Anchor.

Sicherman, Barbara, and Carol Hurd Green, eds., with Ilene Kantrov and Harriette Walker. *Notable American Women: The Modern Period: A Biographical Dictionary.* 1980. Cambridge: The Belknap Press of Harvard University Press.

Sherr, Lynn, and Jurete Kuzickas. 1994. *Susan B. Anthony Slept Here: A Guide to Women's Landmarks.* New York: Random House.

Spender, Dale. 1986. *Mothers of the Novel: 100 Good Women Writers Before Jane Austen.* London and New York: Pandora.

Trager, James. 1994. *The Women's Chronology: A Year-by-Year Record, From Prehistory to the Present.* New York: Henry Holt.

Vare, Ethlie Ann, and Greg Ptacek. 1988. *Mothers of Invention: From the Bra to the Bomb, Forgotten Women and Their Unforgettable Ideas.* New York: Morrow, William and Co. Inc.

Wilms, Denise, and Ilene Cooper. 1987. *A Guide to Non-Sexist Children's Books, Vol II 1976–1985.* Chicago: Academy Chicago Publishers.